BUYING JUST LIKE
THE ANCIENT GREEKS

Buying Just Like the Ancient Greeks

What ancient Greek purchasing can teach us about procurement now

Bob Soames

Buy Research Publications

ISBN 978–0–9551790–9–9

Printed in Great Britain
by
Imprint Digital, Exeter

To Linda, Richard and Jamie

Contents

Foreword

by Sir Anthony Cleaver MA, FBCS, Hon FCIPS

When Bob Soames asked if I would write a Foreword for this book, my first reaction was that I was not qualified to do so. The Chartered Institute of Purchasing and Supply had made me an Honorary Fellow when I was leading IBM. I then became Chairman of the UKAEA (where Bob had purchasing responsibilities) but I have never been a professional purchaser. As for my Greek, it is exactly fifty years since I read Greek at Oxford and my only reading in the original in recent years has been Homer who, as far as I can recall, provides no evidence on this topic – unless you consider Bellerophon's σηματα λυγρα[1] the small print of a Mafia-style contract.

By contrast, Bob has enjoyed a long and distinguished career in procurement, and in recent years has researched and found considerable amounts of evidence to support the main thesis of this book. His literary sources range from observations by Herodotos and Thucydides via Plato and Aristotle to more detailed references in Demosthenes and Theophrastos. For much of the detail, however, the evidence is literally written in stone and he has drawn widely on the epigraphic sources which have been so well collated in recent years.

No doubt procurement professionals will have their own views on some of the contractual issues discussed, while Greek scholars

---

[1] Bellerophron did not read the small print. The σηματα λυγρα ('weasel words' might be a suitable translation in this context) in the closed tablet he was asked to hand to his hosts instructed them to kill him. (*Iliad* Book 6.)

may debate some of the interpretations advanced, but for me, and I suspect most readers, the fundamental thesis is both surprising and illuminating for us today. When I was growing up, "The Greeks had a word for it" was a common expression. Bob's claim is that, in the case of purchasing, the Greeks actually had a process that any modern purchasing professional would recognise – and one that in one major respect was arguably superior to current practice.

The period covered by this study is fairly clearly bounded. Commercial contracting on any serious scale cannot be evidenced until both writing and money became established in society, so there is little to draw on before the fifth century BCE. Equally, given that this is specifically a study of Greek practice, around 150 BCE the Graeco-Roman period takes over. Similarly the author does not cover the practice in other contemporary societies such as Egypt, not least because in his view the process observed is heavily dependent on the nature of the Greek states in which it is found.

The number of parallels with current practices I found surprising, with the author's asides on recent problems in our society, from MPs' expenses to the financial crisis, particularly telling. From the growth of outsourcing to detailed points such as the requirement for oral witnesses despite the presence of the written contract, the parallels are legion. And, as a past member of the Committee on Standards in Public Life, I fully endorse the emphasis on transparency – the key area where we still have a long way to go to match the Greeks.

As one who has always felt truly fortunate to have had a classical education, I was delighted to find yet another area where we can usefully learn from ancient Greece.

Preface

*"The ancient Greeks teach us how to do procurement now?"
That's ridiculous! Life is totally different now. Of course, I'm
not an expert, though I know they were a clever lot and all kinds
of things we now do have their origins in what they did; but
procurement . . . . Of course, they invented 'democracy' and
they must have worked out how to build their great temples and
towns somehow, but didn't the elites just tell servants and slaves
what to do?"*

I read Greek and Latin at university before going into business,
ending up specialising in procurement. And though I have always
known quite a lot more about the ancient Greeks than many
people do, and I kept up my interest in my spare time, I didn't
know much about how they did business until, after a chance
meeting and conversation, I started to read specialist books. To
be honest, I didn't really know anything – and it had never really
occurred to me.

This little book is about what I discovered. Much more was
familiar than I had expected, and what started as a few notes
became much longer. I read many erudite and scholarly works
on ancient Greek contract law, economics, trade, banking, etc.
Since I was a student, there has been an explosion of interest,
especially in continental Europe, in the wider areas of ancient
Greek economics, trade and commerce, all of which is very
relevant to the study of ancient procurement.

However, with one possible exception (a scholarly study

written over forty years ago, *The Greek Temple Builders at Epidaurus* by Alison Burford), I have come across nothing which in my view addresses in one place the totality of the processes involved in acquiring goods and services, etc., which those in the procurement profession nowadays call 'procurement'. Yet I established to my satisfaction that the ancient Greeks must have approached planning, specifying, sourcing and acquisition in ways that were often remarkably similar, in principle, to modern 'best practice' procurement.

There was, however, one significant difference: unlike us, they had no concept of confidentiality. In fact they even published their 'public sector' contracts so that everyone could see the detail of what had been agreed.

Something else was very interesting, though I would not wish to push the argument too far. I think it is possible to trace the origin of some of today's business problems with countries such as Iraq and Afghanistan, especially in respect of what the 'West' regards as corrupt ways of using contract monies, to the reality that by (very roughly) 500BCE, the way in which the Greeks thought about contract process had begun to differ markedly from that of their contemporaries.

I therefore decided to try to bring together in one place, and in as accessible a way as I could, what we know of what the ancient Greeks did, compare it with modern practice, and see if the outcome gives us any food for thought; or maybe just a short book which present day managers can read as a quirky curiosity or as light relief from their day-to-day responsibilities.

Although my main target readership for this book are procurement specialists like myself, what we try to do is not always well known outside the business community. I therefore hope the book may help to inform those who might have a passing interest in procurement and also anyone curious about aspects of ancient business, including perhaps some classical scholars.

Procurement practices are quite frequently presented in the media today as the cause of financial, industrial and social disputes. What is involved at a practical level, how it comes about, and why some of the problems which can happen do happen, is likely to be reasonably topical and will probably remain so for the foreseeable future.

Nowadays I specialise in professional skills training for procurement. I keep my skills up-to-date by seeing a wide range of different contracts, from both the public and private sectors. I find that all too often simple mistakes and errors are made which could easily be avoided with a little more thought and planning. This book might remind readers of why we should do things in a particular way, and what the fundamental issues are. I have not held back from commenting on what, in my view, is sloppy modern practice, though I would be the first to recognise that this often occurs not just because of the complexity and range of all the topics which need to be managed (though this is a real problem) but also because setting up and running cost-efficient contracts requires more resource, skill (and good fortune) than is usually allowed for.

It is my personal (and I am sure, in some places, indulgent) attempt to address all of this from a perspective that interested me. Maybe readers, as they read about the procurement realities of ancient Greece, will find it interesting too. And, more importantly to my mind, maybe it will help us all to re-consider whether the ways of doing things we take for granted are in fact the best or the only ways.

Just as I was finishing, the then Conservative opposition announced that if elected they would demand greater procurement transparency. In May 2010 they became part of a coalition government, and on 5th June 2010 that government announced their plans for the online disclosure of all central government spending and contracts above £25,000, and for council contracts in England and Wales above £500. Guidance on all this has been published, and it will be interesting to see what actually happens as we move through 2011, and if this change helps to redress the excessive adherence to business confidentiality that I suspect is at the core of some of the problems of trust and openness in society as a whole between those who have, and those who have less.

Making the right business decisions in the heat of the moment and being prepared to face one's critics in the marketplace has always been difficult. Did the Greeks, who appear to have done business in ways which are similar to much modern contract practice, but who practised a remarkable degree of transparency, get it right every time, or did they, like us, have feet of clay?

Bob Soames BA, Cert Field Arch, FCIPS
February 2011

Further information

This book is a summary of my researches and I take full responsibility for the errors that have no doubt survived attempts at correction. I have reduced to a minimum detailed references to the books I read and the hundreds of ancient contracts and other sources I have considered and assessed. In the interests of transparency these sources are recorded and maintained, with a full Bibliography and with detailed references, in a version of the text which may interest classical scholars researching aspects of these areas. For more information contact:

bobsoames@contractsconsultancy.co.uk

Acknowledgements

Thanks to:

Professor Lene Rubinstein, MA (Copenhagen), PhD (Cantab), Royal Holloway College, University of London. It was the conversation I had with Lene, after I had attended a lecture she had given on ancient accountability, at a conference for teachers of Latin and Greek, which started me on this. It led to further exchanges and I am very grateful to her for help and guidance, including on where to look for evidence, and her forbearance of my methods.

Professor Peter J Rhodes MA, D Phil, FBA, now Honorary Professor of Ancient History at the University of Durham, was also kind enough to read a draft and make valuable comments.

Mr Nigel Shaw FCIPS, C Eng, FICE, MIMechE (and amongst other distinguished services to procurement, Chairman of the NEC Panel of the Institution of Civil Engineers, tasked with overseeing the continuing evolution of the internationally used and acclaimed NEC family of contract conditions) also most kindly read through the whole book and commented on some modern-day aspects.

Sir Anthony Cleaver MA, FBCS, Hon FCIPS, etc., was Chairman of IBM UK and then the United Kingdom Atomic Energy Authority, later becoming first Chairman of the Nuclear Decommissioning Authority. I am most grateful to him for writing the Foreword to this book. Sir Anthony was President of the Classical Association in 1995/6 and amongst many public appointments was a member of the Wicks Committee on Standards in Public Life. Until recently he was Chairman of Engineering UK, which aims to inspire people at all levels to pursue careers in engineering and technology.

The staff of the Institute of Classical Studies Library, Joint Library of the Hellenic and Roman Societies, University of London School of Advanced Study, for their help in tracking down elusive epigraphical texts.

Background

Bob Soames read Classics at Bristol University and joined the United Kingdom Atomic Energy Authority where he gained extensive experience in many areas of management, eventually specialising in Procurement (which he headed), later becoming a Fellow of the Chartered Institute of Purchasing and Supply.

He is now a consultant and trainer in procurement and project management, and a member of CIPS' Contracts Specialist Group. Returning to his roots, he is again studying the ancient Greek world.

1

INTRODUCTION
AND APPROACH

There are many scholarly studies of commercial activities in ancient Greece. The direct evidence available for study is relatively limited, as in all forms of ancient history. What evidence there is has usually been considered from the perspective of what legal or economic/trading information can be identified from the surviving records. One might well ask, 'but how else?' This book attempts to review the material from a slightly different angle – from the perspective of a modern English practitioner of the art (if in fact it is an art) of professional procurement, and who is also interested in whether we modern procurement practitioners can learn from ancient practices. This may appear to cut across recognised approaches; cause and effect may be mixed up, and the methodology adopted might be criticised on the grounds that it risks – perhaps even encourages – anachronistic interpretation. Such a charge is very hard to deny, given that the primary reason for approaching the issues this way is the author's perhaps surprising assumption that modern practitioners may perceive commercial matters with, in a very limited way, something of the same mindset of the ancient Greeks in the same line of business, and that this will enable some new insight. But of course, so much is so utterly different from 2,500 years ago.

However, what did become clear, the more the work developed, were the parallels, even similarities, between the way things are now done (despite so many years and cultural changes) and what the Greeks had developed to meet their commercial and societal needs. At one level this is obvious and inevitable – risk and reward in business is bound to be some combination of carrot and stick for those involved – but it was the closeness of the similarities that was surprising, allowing always for the limited amount of evidence which enables such an assessment to be made.

Much of the literary evidence we have comes from Athens. However, the epigraphic record – ancient inscriptions, often on stone, but including inscriptions on other media (e.g., lead, pottery [ostraka], wood, wax tablets, papyrus, etc.) – comes from all over the ancient Greek world. This means we may have evidence from southern Spain, France and Italy, modern day Turkey and the Black Sea coasts, and Egypt as well as what we still call Greece itself.

At the present time of writing the 'Western' mercantilist approach to business is in the ascendant. Although the world of the ancient Greeks was in so many ways very different from ours, they seem to have been to some extent 'proto-Western mercantilists' so the kinds of issues they faced were not so different. More importantly for present purposes, the outcome of the ways they addressed these issues seems often to have resulted in solutions remarkably similar to those we use nowadays, and we use essentially the same tools as they did. In fact there appears to be very little new in this area since the time of the Greek city states. Whether this is the result of independent development in response to similar problems, or, for example, whether there are direct transmission links to be discerned, is outside my scope. The extent to which the tools and techniques used in ancient Greek procurement involved innovation by the Greeks, or perhaps the development of even earlier practices, is interesting, but speculative; and I have not resisted the temptation to put forward some ideas when it seemed appropriate.

My approach involves touching lightly over a range of topics rather than drilling deeply into particular areas, as might be the case in a research project. This, however, is in line with the essence of the modern professional approach to procurement, which perceives the supply-chain process as a whole and tries to establish how best to package up, in a way which will align with what is available in the marketplace, the requirements of colleagues who ask for items or services not available 'in house'. The major changes in procurement practice and perceptions of procurement that have occurred in recent years amongst leading commercial organisations are a result of this supply-chain perspective.

Many of the modern supply-chain techniques that have been adopted were pioneered by companies with significant UK interests, and the British public sector also has significant involvement. The manner in which leading organisations organise to procure often differs from the everyday practice in more traditional companies, and throughout the world there continues to be a significant diversity in procurement processes.

In one area in particular the ancient Greek approach was very different to ours. The Greeks do not appear to have had any concept of commercial confidentiality. In their 'public sector' at least, the Greeks did not seek to keep confidential the details of their contracts. Management structures, specifications, terms and conditions, pay and prices were deliberately made available for the man in the street to see and read. The significance of this is not so much the extent to which the 'ancient Greek in the market place' may or may not have read and understood these details – we have no means of knowing this – but the effect it may have had on how individuals (and their business enterprises) carried out their obligations to their fellow citizens, and also the extent to which public practice may, however indirectly, have influenced contractual behaviours between individuals acting solely in a private capacity.

It may even be that reflecting on this practice could help prompt some modern day business and procurement practitioners to think through and to question what has nowadays become the generally accepted (and therefore perhaps comfortable) practice of assuming, almost automatically, that it is inevitable that all detailed contract information should in principle be regarded as commercially confidential rather than, in principle, available to all. The EC Procurement Directives and Freedom of Information legislation are modern day attempts to make business more transparent in the huge area of public sector contracting, and initially they made some progress. However, it seems to me that any benefits gained now risk being lost. Legal and bureaucratic wrangling over the interpretation of the statutes often obscures the fundamental intention of the contract as a whole. At the same time many contracts seem to be getting longer and more complex, ostensibly in the cause of greater clarity and better defined risk (excellent objectives in themselves), albeit that all too often in practice, even if the parties were to agree to forgo commercial confidentiality, only the specialist few would easily be able to understand the provisions.

I would not for a moment argue that there is no need at all for some commercial confidentiality, but I suspect that the overall effect of these trends in business has been a loss of trust in public accountability and officialdom. After I started my researches, the enforced lifting (in 2008/9) of the veil of confidentiality around UK MPs' expenses and the salaries of bankers (and others) has drawn further attention to these issues. The smooth running of our modern Western political systems depends upon a consensus among people and politicians that the forms of democracy we operate are broadly in everyone's long-term interest. As political commentators have noted, too large a disconnection of interest between leaders and led risks a breakdown in these relationships. I am not sure that sufficient attention has yet been drawn to the wider societal implications of excessive commercial confidentiality.

In the 1990s there were two notable developments against these trends. Firstly, many governments in the West sought to enhance and extend access to the internet – making this a key governmental objective. And, secondly, a decision was reached at supra-national level to make available freely the full results of the Human Genome Project. Overall however, and crucially at the practical level, the trend is the other way. All too often, and long after the event, contract audits have shown that excessive confidentiality can be a refuge for sloppy thinking and partisan or fraudulent activity. Perhaps the contractual practices which were part of the route to the 2008 banking crisis are an example; I have not yet heard or read of anyone who claims to have understood fully all the implications of the 'toxic' contracts.

2

THE BACKGROUND
– GREEK AND MODERN.
WHAT IS PURCHASING?

Modern purchasing has often been regarded as a fairly simple transactional activity and associated with clerical support. Over the past thirty or so years, however, it has become more generally accepted that major procurements are essentially a process, typically involving a number of different stakeholders and a number of distinct phases. Major procurement, or strategic procurement, seen as a process will involve technical, financial and supply risk assessment, considerable flexibility and often significant innovative thinking.

How did the ancient Greeks look upon purchasing? Like us, probably most people never gave that question a moment's thought, but some literary evidence very broadly connected to purchasing activity does survive. Two short works by the late 5th century BCE author Xenophon survive — the *Economics* and the *Ways and Means*. The philosophers Plato and Aristotle also mention purchasing matters, largely incidentally in their works. It is possible that someone may once have attempted to codify purchasing processes in some written form; if so nothing of it survives.

Nevertheless, from other records we can discern a surprising amount about ancient approaches to this activity. A key factor in this is to understand something of the nature of the Greek approach to the very idea of commercial relationships. The French scholar Alain Bresson, in his book *La Cité Marchande*, neatly summarised his insight of the key points of the ancient Greek developments, as they influenced procurement practice as follows:

In the world of [the Greek] cities, it was buying and selling which ruled the circulation of goods. This market principle was the glue which enabled all free men to come to a deal which had full legal effect. In the same way, it was possible to execute freely a contract which would have absolute legal effect in the body of the community where it had been established and which would eventually also be able to have a form of legal recognition in other cities. In the business arena, the contract ... was an essential element in the social functioning of the Greek city. Certainly, the notion of contract is not specific to Greece. Babylonia or Pharaonic Egypt are themselves also known to have a system of contract which, in its form, is not far removed from that which applied in Greece. But it wasn't an essential; the difference between the Greek world and the world of empires is the fact that in Greece all free men were subject to the terms of a contract with universal legal validity, while in Babylon or in Egypt the decisions of the prince could make null and void a whole contract in all its particulars. Moreover, in the world of the Greek cities, a contract had full and entire legal validity even if it was executed by a foreigner, and the fact that the contractor was Greek (or not) did not give him any especial rights. The system of how business was carried out which was put in place in Athens in 4th century was the completion point of a fundamental issue, which is that this type of process would not be judged by the function of the individual but the function of the nature of the case.' [My translation.]

The proposal in the last sentence of the quotation, that process takes precedence over the role and interests of any single individual, is the key point. It represents a major cultural shift in society. When and how that change will have taken place is not known. Certainly it is difficult to envisage any real life equivalents of the kinds of individuals depicted in the antique Greek world – e.g., the Homeric heroes of the Trojan war stories (Achilles, Hector, Agamemnon, Odysseus, etc.) accepting restrictions to their individual freedoms as a result of a law passed by an assembly. Something affecting their notion of honour or personal responsibility was a different matter, and of course, a decision taken as a result of a personal judgement that it might be unwise to ignore views expressed by one's followers is different again.

Conventionally in Greek historiography, the 'age of the lawgivers' is broadly late 7th and the 6th century BCE and, although most surviving evidence of contractual agreements involving individuals dates from the 4th century, there is enough earlier material for us to be sure that the cultural shift Bresson postulates occurred before the beginning of the 5th century. This is interesting as recently, undoubtedly as a response to continuing Middle-Eastern inspired terrorist problems, some popular historians have suggested that the beginning of the 5th century BCE (culminating in the Greek victory over the Persians at Marathon in 490BCE and the further victories ten years later) is a defining era as it was then that the 'West' parted company with the 'East'. Whether making so clear a distinction is justifiable is not a matter for this book, but media reports in recent years about the way monies provided for contracts have been spent in Afghanistan and other parts of the world have drawn attention to the differences there are between the cultural assumptions of 'Western' countries and those in other parts of the world. Could it be that an underlying consequence of the way the Greeks chose to approach contractual process 2,500 years ago is still resonating across the world today?

There was another major cultural change that took place in the Greek world (again the precise dates are uncertain but the practical outcome was clear by the beginning of the 5th century) which may have had an equally important influence on business practice. This was the development of money, and especially the development of money from being a relatively simple concept — as 'bullion' enabling cash transactions — towards seeing it as a token of value, or indeed, as we do nowadays, as merely a concept of fiducial value regardless of its 'real' presence in any particular transaction (fiduciary money). How and why this development came about, like the implications for commerce of legal structure, are currently areas of discussion amongst scholars and it would be interesting to identify which came first, and which influenced the other more or less. However, neither of these issues is explicitly relevant for this book. The key point for us is the possibility that the concurrence of the two developing concepts could have catalysed the behaviourial change which led to the development of contractual business as a normal process in the Greek world.

Ancient Greece comprised autonomous 'city states'; there was not a single nation. Contracts made at city state to city state level were therefore rather like state-to-state treaties, conventions, multilateral agreements, etc., and are therefore different in kind from contracts which involve states and individuals — 'public sector' contracts in our terms — and wholly 'private sector' contracts (the rest). I have in principle ignored state-to-state agreements in this book on the grounds that such arrangements have always existed, both when 'kings' embodying in themselves a state made a deal with other similar 'kings', or when states (as we know them today) negotiate with other states. These are not business deals as most practitioners would see them. Our interest is with contracts below this 'governmental' level. However, whereas kings and states have by virtue of their status nearly unlimited resources to record and publicise their activities should they so wish, it might at first sight appear unlikely that records of less prestigious contracts would survive 2,500 years. Fortunately, the nature of the Greek approach to the contractual process is such that some evidence does still exist.

The economic environment in which the Greeks did business was also a critical part of the developing commercial world in which the first contracts — as we might recognise them — came into being. Discussion about the sophistication and nature of the ancient economy has been a very disputed area among scholars for many years and is not for discussion here. Suffice it to note that currently the debate has moved towards a more nuanced understanding of the ancient Greek economy which fits well with the relatively complex and sophisticated procurement practices (at least by the 4th century) which I have identified.

The increasingly widespread use of cash would have been a major enabling factor in this regard, and evidence has been found for this in the cash economy in 4th century Athens. However, the pre-eminence of money in exchange is probably not essential for a developed economy which uses contracts. I live in the Berkshire Downs in a village only twenty miles from Oxford but have found (initially to my surprise but not now, after twenty-five years) that non-financial commerce, albeit marginally used, can still be a feature of daily life. The human animal's capacity to achieve its survival and further objectives in spite of official mechanisms and systems seems to be infinite, so where there is a lack of specific evidence for particular practices in Greek commerce it can perhaps be regarded more as a gap in the evidence than a certainty that the practice did not exist. As new research uncovers new evidence, so the sheer variety of practice, and the need to accept that there may not be patterns and recognisable 'systems', can be better appreciated. (Although it remains essential to avoid transferring the cultural values implicit in 21st century Western civilisation to the ancient world, it might be that in 2011, with some of the previous norms of the early 21st century financial world now contentious, non-financial commerce may be due for something of a resurgence.)

Virtually everyone is a buyer or purchaser at some level, but apparently innate personal skills or aptitudes, and learnt techniques — e.g., 'wheeler/dealer' skills, or legal knowledge — make some more successful than others. There is no reason to believe that this facet of human nature was vastly different in antiquity. While evidence for commercial and trading relations goes back to the Minoan period in Crete and beyond, on the basis of my own professional experience what constitutes real commercial practice (in any age) certainly seems to be more than the apparent sum of its parts. Commercial practice comprises a mix of what we might describe as 'primary skills', i.e. pragmatic 'tradesman-like' knowledge (e.g., to buy construction well, some understanding of what a bricklayer or a Quantity Surveyor actually does on site is needed) but also 'back office practices' — e.g., accounting, banking and legal knowledge. The evidence for primary skills beyond a superficial level is unlikely to be preserved even by the most advanced archaeological techniques. However, literary or epigraphic records preserve some of the back office knowledge.

Unfortunately, as implied above, there is in addition the fact that much of what is involved in a commercial transaction does not keep. The reality of procurement is that it is a special relationship between people which is aimed at the achievement of a particular objective. It is of no lasting value outside the small group involved. In Britain today, even in the public sector where retention of contractual records is legally required (and where organisations are commonly assumed to be sufficiently competent to comply with the law — an assumption often at odds with the reality in this area), 80% or more of modern contracts are routinely destroyed after two years, and 99% of the remainder are destroyed six years after they end. Space does not allow otherwise. Perversely — according to a report in *The Observer* newspaper of 25th January 2009 — the Head of the British Library feared that the ubiquity of rapidly changing standards of IT media may mean that even copies of what may be intentionally retained, if not in paper form, may well become inaccessible if the technology needed to read them no longer exists.

A further problem is that what is written down is often no more than what is required to meet legal or organisational requirements — some signed documents and perhaps a few formal notes and exchanges between the parties; it is not the essence of the relationship. What may be left from this mass destruction are the details of the very few contracts which went so wrong or were so unusual that, exceptionally, they were retained, or which escaped destruction through sheer chance.

Although the comments above about commercial transactions are universal, fortunately — for the purposes of any study of procurement processes — ancient Greek society, especially in democracies, required public record keeping in much the same way as we do nowadays. By the 4th century at least, there were sophisticated public record keeping practices at Athens. No doubt many early records were on wood or papyrus and other formats which do not keep, but gradually much came to be on stone, and enough of this epigraphic evidence has survived to make informed assessments possible. And a proportion of what does survive is contractual or has potential links to procurements.

Fortunately too, there are quite a number of similar epigraphic survivals from all over the Greek speaking world, covering the period from about the 6th century BCE to the present era. Thus we can still read some ancient Greek contract documents, and take a view about (what we would call) public sector contracts; and from that perhaps extrapolate something about contracts where there was no state involvement, especially as some partial examples of this category also survive. (The use of the terms 'public sector' and 'private sector' does not make accurate sense in respect of ancient Greek contracts – nor do they always in respect of modern day contracting – but I use the terms throughout in this book as shorthand to distinguish between the two broad categories described above.)

There are also literary sources, mostly composed during the period from roughly 430-330BCE. The philosophers, Plato and Aristotle especially, discuss matters relevant to procurement, and there is some relevant information in the historians and other authors. The orators, particularly Demosthenes, are a major source of information, though most of the contractual arrangements with which they are concerned are what we would classify as banking loans and insurances, which are not typically the everyday concern of most 21st century procurement specialists. Many of the relevant surviving speeches are about disputes between private individuals, so we do obtain 'non-public sector' information. However, this material is not necessarily robust since (as on reflection one might expect) an oration in the law courts was about constructing a legal or political case, not recording objectively the full details of a contractual transaction. Moreover, none of the surviving writers was writing a treatise on procurement as such. (A work called the *Economika*[1] is the nearest to this, but it seems to me that the real procurement element in it is incidental). Taken as a whole however, a possibly surprising amount of information can be gleaned from all these sources.

Certainly there is enough to enable one to ask interesting questions such as:

---

[1] The author, once thought to have been Aristotle, is unknown. It is usually still published with collections of Aristotle's work.

a) Did the Greeks think of procurement as a process, or just a transactional activity?

b) Did different types of purchasing attract different approaches?

c) Why were Greek practices so different from ours as regards commercial confidentiality and publicity for contracts?

d) Did the Greeks use sub-contractors?

e) Were outsourcing practices such as outsourcing tax collection ('tax farming' — the 'publicans' of the King James' Bible) the result of a deliberate choice to limit the activities of what we would now call the central bureaucracy, or are there other reasons? Could this be a model for us to follow?

f) Does the evidence, taken as a whole, provide information which, if communicated more widely, might have relevance to those dealing with procurement issues now, 2,500 years later?

I attempt some answers to these questions later in this book. First, though, is it possible to define what procurement (or purchasing) is? It might be surprising to learn that the definition of the acquisition process, apparently so simple and fundamental a part of everyday living, especially in the 21st century, is still the subject of considerable debate, not only in academic circles but amongst practitioners. But this, however, is the case. The problems have arisen in the UK as a result of the way the use of the words has developed and changed over the past fifty years or so. Is it Procurement or Purchasing, or Buying, or Contracts, or Commercial? Yet different terminology again is now used in some business sectors. Definitions have also depended, to a certain extent, upon whether organisations choose to set up separate structures to carry out this work. It has also been influenced by the personal career paths of the individuals leading these structures. However, these niceties are of marginal interest from the perspective of anyone studying the acquisition process of 2,500 years ago. Their problem is primarily the paucity of evidence generally. I therefore use the words in the following way:

Commercial — a broad term used to cover the buying and selling aspects of business.

Procurement — thinking out and planning what to purchase and how to purchase it.

Supply Chain — all the stages which comprise the processes involved in identifying and undertaking a Procurement, from obtaining raw material through manufacturing, supply, installation, maintenance and taking out of use/demolition to final disposal.

Purchase/Purchasing — the act of buying, obtaining via barter or consideration/monies but especially via a written contract.

Buying — obtaining small commodities/daily shopping.

Contracts/Contracting — the legally enforceable and apparently agreed outcome of a sale/purchase negotiation. Often a 'piece of paper' containing the specifications, terms, conditions etc. (The diminutive of Contract is **order**, which is linked to buying, not purchasing.)

Sale/s — the act of selling, either by barter or consideration/ monies.

A modern, simple but comprehensive definition of the whole procurement process from a current textbook is:

The process undertaken by the organisational unit that, either as a function, or as part of an integrated supply chain, is responsible for procuring or assisting users to procure, in the most efficient manner, required supplies at the right time, quality, quantity, and price and the management of suppliers, thereby contributing to the competitive advantage of the enterprise, and the achievement of its corporate strategy.[1]

This definition has no especial merit except its currency and conscious attempt at being comprehensive. For my purposes, however, it is a sufficiently good definition of 21st century practice to provide the measure against which to assess ancient practice.

The essence of the definition is that something, probably a physical supply, is procured, but it could be something less tangible, like a service. There are, of course, many kinds of service contract possible, including financial loan services (from, e.g., banks). Most procurement specialists regard such contracts as 'banking', not procurement, and although I touch on banking practices below, and draw on ancient evidence from banking, in principle I regard bank loan contracts as outside the scope of this book. (There are now many procurement specialists working in the financial sector. By and large they procure goods and services for the bankers; they do not expect to do 'banking'. Whether the financial world now would be in a different place if typical procurement considerations such as 'full lifetime cost of the procurement strategy' and 'cost of making good' applied to 'banking' contracts is an interesting speculation).

Certain key words have to be translated to make sense. Thus:

'Organisational unit' and 'enterprise' in principle mean 'the same corporate entity' (and the whole question of 'corporateness' is an issue itself).

For 'users' read: 'those who have the need for the service, goods, etc.' They are often known as 'Customers', or sometimes 'Clients' as they pay, either directly or indirectly, for the service.

'Corporate strategy' in these terms is the plan to achieve the end product of the procurement process. In these terms we might nowadays (with the full benefit of hindsight) look upon the completion of the Parthenon project (for example) as an end

---

[1] Lysons, K, and Farrington, B, *Purchasing and Supply Management*, 7th edition, 2006 (Pearson Education) p. 8.

product within Pericles' overall corporate strategy for Athens' glorification. 'Suppliers' are contractors.

While to the best of my knowledge no equivalent Greek 'management-speak' definition of Procurement or Purchasing (or, for that matter, 'Sale' has survived), there is more than enough evidence in the sources for us to be sure that the words for buying and selling, and the other more technical words also used to cover the various parts of the activity, were well understood in ancient times. The problem, as always in all such matters, is to try to understand what the parties at the time may have hoped to convey by the words they used when they used them. Fairly recently one scholar dissected possible interpretations in the context of, principally, surviving ὅροι (*horoi*) (mortgage contract) inscriptions, and established that, often, the meanings depended upon the perspective of the writer. A consequence of this is that, as my 'purchase' is your 'sale', the same words can have apparently diametrically opposite meanings, depending upon context. However, he also, crucially, pointed out that Greek law was much more flexible than the later Roman law was to be. Roman law is the basis of much of our modern legal practice and is thus our often unintentional mindset. It is not that 'words mean what I choose them to mean', but there is an element of this. Thus, for purchase or sale, the ancient Greek words are (at least): ἀγοραζω (*agorazo*) — I am a frequenter of the market place, hence I buy; but most often ὠνεομαι/πριαμαι (*oneomai/priamai*) — I buy.

The Greek word most often used for selling is πολεω (*poleo*) — I sell, or more explicitly, I exchange or barter goods (which can mean buying as well as selling). ἀποδιδωμι (*apodidomi*) is also used.

Further subtleties in meaning create difficulties if one tries to over-define. For example, there are a number of frequently used Greek words which can be translated as 'contract', but how they are used depends on a number of factors. Their use also developed and changed over time and place so that what can be translated as meaning broadly what we would now call a commercial contract may be more nuanced in a precise context. In the light this, I do not attempt to define precisely.

How curious it is that, as indicated above, we have very similar problems of terminology nowadays.

3

METHOD STATEMENT, AND A BRIEF PERSONAL VIEW OF THE HISTORY OF MODERN BRITISH PROCUREMENT

The ancient Greek historian Thucydides made a timeless comment about human endeavour 2,500 years ago when, commenting on his reasons for writing history he said:

> It will be enough for me if these words of mine are judged useful by those who want to understand clearly the events which happened in the past and which (human nature being what it is) will, at some time or other, and in much the same ways, be repeated in the future.

These words probably sum up all historians' motivations when attempting to understand the past. It was during Thucydides' lifetime (middle to late 5th century BCE) that many of the developing procurement practices of the Greeks discussed below came to maturity.

The period this book covers lasted a little less than 400 years. This encompasses what we know as the classical period of ancient Greek history – roughly the end of the Persian wars (480BCE) to 322BCE, the death of Alexander the Great. Major changes followed Alexander, and this is called the Hellenistic age. By about 150BCE there were further major changes. This is roughly the time at which the increasing influence of Rome on the Greek speaking world may be judged to mean that what we previously regarded as Greek only becomes Graeco-Roman. I have, therefore, in principle (though not always in practice) chosen 150BCE approximately as the end point for evidence and of any detailed commentary. I have also excluded Eygpt from my considerations, partly in order to keep this to manageable proportions, but mainly because throughout the period, and even after Alexander's time when Greek-speaking Ptolemys ruled Egypt, Egypt's ways of doing things differed from those of the Greek world generally.

The methodology I have used is to compare and contrast in broad terms what applies now with what we can surmise and interpret from the evidence in the sources. I discuss the surviving epigraphical evidence for contracts in some detail as, despite its shortcomings, it is perhaps the most specific and clear kind of evidence that we have for a contract. A close reading of the definition of 'procurement' in Chapter 2 will, however, show that the word 'contract' does not appear at all. The word 'process' does though, and (as indicated in my initial discussion of Bresson's definition) I hold that the process of procurement has to be a relationship between two parties who have the legal right to make or break the contract. Finding explicit evidence for concepts such as processes and relationships 2,500 years ago is, though, a near impossible task, so I cover this ground primarily on a 'by analogy' basis.

Given that the evidence that we have is limited, to restrict one's choice of options yet further might seem perverse, but as indicated above I have deliberately excluded from consideration, as much as is practicable, evidence of business between states and concentrated on areas where at least one party is what we now call a private individual. However, there is a sense in which the private/public distinctions we make in the 21st century would make no sense at all in the ancient Greek world. Throughout the classical and Hellenistic periods, each individual's sense of identity was defined more by their personal relationship to their city and city state than we can easily understand in our increasingly casual relationship (perhaps for some ex-patriate internationalists, even just contractual relationship) with the state in which we happen to reside (and where we may happen to be employed).

There is a further aspect of this ancient relationship issue which is worth mentioning. Until fairly recently there tended to be a generally accepted view amongst scholars that in ancient Greek commerce it was those without citizen status, rather than citizens themselves, who took the lead in business matters. The reason given for this was that because non-citizens were effectively outside the benefits and constraints of their birth-state they were therefore free to (or more realistically, had no option but to) seek their survival via trade. This was because resident non-citizens in city states (often known as metics) and freed slaves (the other main non-citizen group) were not usually allowed to own land and normally also had to pay additional taxes. For them, commerce would have been the obvious way to support themselves. However, more detailed analysis of citizen occupations recently has suggested that numbers of citizens were also deeply involved in commerce; as a result the overall pattern is much less clear than it was. As citizenship status was linked to the idea that a citizen lived off the produce of his own land, and in most ancient Greek city states there was not enough cultivable land for this to work, it was inevitable that many of the less well-to-do citizens had to find other ways to support their families. Commerce, in its various forms, would have been an obvious option.

However, one must also be very careful not to make a simple but anachronistic parallel with modern Britain where it is an accepted notion that immigrant families, having acquired wealth (e.g., by trade) over the generations, transmuted into landowning families, indistinguishable from those who had lived here for very much longer. It is not in fact quite that simple in Britain even now, though our process to obtain formal political rights is fairly easy. Full citizenship (political rights) in ancient Greece was more complex than under our system. For a start, it was not available at all to the founding generation. However, the idea that wealth generation is more often the province of the active and agile among those who have lacked material comforts, rather than of those who already have such benefits (and who may have the leisure to write about it!) may not be too far from the mark.

If we nowadays attempt to analyse and understand business activity, we tend to use particular categories which leaders in business have developed over time, mainly on the basis of what seems to work. We have no means of knowing if the ancients used similar processes, but it does not seem unreasonable that we might assume that what works for us in business, to some extent holds good for the way they worked, albeit they would not categorise things in the way we do or perhaps at all. It is tempting also to suggest that their ways of working may have been more holistic and fluid than ours have become, where 'silo-management' attitudes (an apparent inability to appreciate cause and effect beyond one's own patch) have all too often led to unfortunate outcomes. Press reports about this problem most usually castigate organisations such as social services and the police for such failings; those with procurement (and no doubt other) experience in all manner of industries will unfortunately have little difficulty in recalling their own local examples. In reality the key factor is probably scale; even Athens was small by comparison with modern day organisations and cities.

It is in this spirit that I comment upon accountancy, banking and other practices. I am no expert in any of these individual specialisms – either present day or ancient Greek. The skill-set of the procurement specialist is to attempt to transcend the boundaries of particular specialisms and areas of studies, and to try to mesh or amalgamate the best and practicable aspects of all so as to evolve a pragmatic solution to the procurement need. If it were not such a mouthful, I would prefer to describe what I do professionally as 'External Resources Facilitation Management' (but would anyone want to understand what 'ERFM Specialist' means, let alone employ one?)

A brief personal view of the history of modern British procurement

Traditionally, it was the manufacturing sector, e.g., the automobile and heavy engineering sectors, who employed 'buyers'. These buyers often bought large numbers of similar components, worked with engineers to meet production targets, and were closely involved in specification writing. Similarly, although the contexts and details are very different, procurement for the armed services has long been seen as a specialist function, as has the 'buyer' role in the retail sector. The heavy engineering, building, oil, gas and utilities sectors used specialists to 'contract for' materials and structures, but elsewhere until the 1980s many organisations most often used their own staff to manufacture or convert materials into finished products. Consequently, as much of the conversion work was done by one of the in-house departments, the need to buy in components or finished products was minimal – often just raw materials. Where more dedicated procurement was necessary, non-specialists usually carried out the tasks, often using lawyers to write contract documents. It is only comparatively recently, with the relentless focus of smaller organisations on what has become known as 'core activities' leading to the maximising of profits through the minimisation of 'non-core' spend, that professional purchasing, especially for services, has generally been recognised as a specialist activity – in, for example, the financial sector and among public sector organisations such as the NHS, police, local authorities, universities and in the Civil Service (outside MOD).

As procurement processes have become subject to more and more specialist health, quality, environmental and legal constraints, the consensus has built up that it is better to have a dedicated professional purchaser rather than rely on whatever skills someone may or may not have as an occasional buyer. In recent years, and so far generally in what we may hope are the exceptional circumstances of the economic cycle which started in 2009, rather than being an unrecognised activity outside specialist areas, good quality procurement skills have suddenly been in demand, especially in the public sector. Finding the right staff with the required knowledge and skills is difficult and the recruitment market for top purchasers has been very tight. Professional purchasers have high profile jobs in the Civil Service, and civil servants and others are encouraged to take professional qualifications. In some parts of the public sector, worthwhile bonuses are awarded to those who attain these qualifications.

This development has come about for many reasons, including the recognition that, provided key project definition skills are obtainable 'in house', it is usually cheaper to rely on the market to identify the best value-for-money approach to a particular need. This has led to the outsourcing of many previously in-house services. Often, it has been found that the original understanding of what was needed was deficient in some way, which led to different ways of specifying the need. From this, as far as the UK government is concerned, has come the idea that it is possible to improve services at less total cost by hiving staff off into Agencies, or even public or privately owned companies who then provide the specified service under contract. 'Facilities Management' was invented to describe this specialist service, and facilities management companies have become everyday names.

Apparently clever financial engineering techniques led to the idea that it would be possible to renew outdated UK infrastructure through, first, Private Finance Initiative (PFI) schemes, and, following the change of government in 1997, through Public/ Private Partnership (PPP) schemes. Broadly, these are long-term infrastructure schemes whereby a contractor, or perhaps a consortium of contractors, takes on a long-term (e.g., five year minimum, sometimes ten times as long) contract to undertake a range of tasks, including perhaps demolishing, building, managing, and/or servicing a major public facility.

At the time of writing (2011), the prospects for the best quality people with practical procurement skills have very significantly improved by comparison with what was traditionally available. However, while there are many examples of good and successful practice, there continue to be regular reports of high profile procurement 'disasters'. The nature of the activity, with its scope for things to go wrong, and the luxury of 20/20 hindsight, makes this inevitable. In 2008, when I was first thinking about this excursus, I thought it was still a little early for the worst excesses of poor or inappropriate outsourcing and PPP schemes to hit the news-stands, but noted that it was certain that there would be such cases in the future.

Two or more years later, and the current downturn will inevitably significantly increase the number of cases, including bringing down what in good times would have been sound schemes. All too often the problems arise from lack of corporate memory (probably now mystified as 'Knowledge Management failures') or the lack of basic commercial skills by those charged with committing over time huge sums of money under contract (see as an example the recent criticism of the policy by the National Audit Office.)[1] The legal arguments after the event may eventually, after the expenditure of much more money with

---

[1] Report by the Comptroller and Auditor General, *Central Government's Management of Service Contracts* (December 2008).

third parties such as lawyers and arbitrators, apportion blame to one or other party, but by then the world will have moved on. If the Greeks had similar problems, perhaps we could learn from them; or at least reflect, yet again, on the truth of Thucydides' comment quoted above.

4

WRITTEN RECORDS
— THE SOURCES OF OUR
INFORMATION

Even in the best managed modern organisations, only limited records are kept of most commercial transactions. They are important at the time, but once the transaction is fully complete – whether to the satisfaction of both parties, or neither – people concentrate on the next deal. This makes trying to understand how people did business more difficult. I know from personal experience, and from procurement colleagues who have audited formal records, that even if they do not know the actual individuals involved, they are able to gauge more accurately than those without such procurement experience, whether a particular contract or decision was likely to have been a good one or not. For those in business, concerned to survive for another day, that is ultimately the only relevant question. Attempting a similar assessment, but trying to look back 2,500 years, is clearly fraught with scope for error, but facing up to the problem is at least a starting point when one comes to read the literary and epigraphical sources for contracts in ancient Greece. It is worth noting that even indirect references to business practice can be helpful as they may reveal attitudes to business which would not be evident in a dedicated account of the topic.

Tracking down the evidence that I have used meant reading many specialist books as well as the ancient authors to whom I have referred. I also had to read, and in most cases translate, as translations do not always exist (and besides, are they right?), the epigraphical evidence I found. Fortunately, many of the actual texts are now available online on the University of Princeton Epigraphical Database, which provides a convenient starting point. Modern procurement readers are unlikely to be interested in these details so they are not included here, though I have available privately a longer version of the book with all this detail explicitly recorded for anyone who is interested.

My use of reference material in respect of aspects of modern procurement is knowingly and intentionally less well documented, and my descriptions and comments are mainly the outcome of my own acquired knowledge and experience rather than being capable of reference to particular academic texts.

The reason that numbers of epigraphical inscriptions setting out individual contract details have survived is because the Greeks practised what we might now term 'open government'. From roughly the 5th century onwards, it was probably the growing influence and sheer size (relative to other cities) of democratic Athens which meant that the practice of having the populace elect officials regularly, and insist by law that what they did on behalf of their electorate be openly recorded, became fairly common throughout Greece. This meant that work could be audited and checked to ensure that the officials carried out their tasks in accordance with policy, and it led to extensive record keeping. Fortunately for researchers nowadays, at around the same time, other city states, including those not necessarily of similar democratic persuasion, also began to record their activities and contracts publicly.

Of course, those epigraphs which have survived have only done so through chance or luck. For example, sometimes the inscribed stones were re-used and hence the writing was protected; on other occasions re-use meant breaking up and greater damage, so that piecing together shattered fragments is the only way some text can be reconstituted. Occasionally, inscriptions have been found more or less in the original place – sufficiently at any rate for us to be able to be certain that the Greeks published the details of contracts in public places – e.g., in the *agora* (market place) or (in the case of mortgage contracts) at the doorpost of the mortgaged estate.

Lead tablets, too, were used for long-term record keeping and a few of these containing 'private sector' contracts have also survived. So have contracts on papyrus, but only in Egypt, which I have excluded from this study. In the same way, recording contracts on wood would have been a frequently used medium for what, at the time, would have been seen as long-term storage of records, but none of these have been found. In the context of record keeping more generally, *ostraka* (scratched potsherds used for generally ephemeral notes) quite frequently survive by virtue of their nature, but the writing surface is very small and I am not aware of any survivals which contain information that can be interpreted as contractual detail.

Of the contracts on stone I have read, some are very inform-ative. On the other hand, as anyone who has seen in a museum what are usually the best preserved examples of inscriptions can immediately appreciate, the legible preservation of sufficient text to be sure of all the detail is rare. Fortunately, enough partial survivals exist to enable a fairly detailed picture to be ascertained, especially because (as is best practice in contracting nowadays) ancient Greek contracts tended to be written using a standard format. It lessens the risk of omitting essential routine information. This means that it has often been feasible for scholars to work out the probable meaning when letters, words or even whole phrases are missing from a text, and thus extend our knowledge by analogy. Even partial survivals have sometimes shed light on issues which are otherwise only implicit in a literary source. With this caveat, the epigraphic record, especially from the fourth to second centuries, provides us with information outside the boundaries of Athens and is a potentially rich source of information.

As will become clear below from the discussion of the evidence that can be gathered and interpreted, nearly all the legal concepts which underlie our 21st century understanding of a contract were established and mature concepts by the time of Alexander the Great (330BCE). The majority of the potential points of dispute between parties which (ideally) have to be resolved in principle beforehand – i.e., what we often systematise as the 'Conditions of Contracts' – had been identified, and models or accepted ways of dealing with the issues, were in force from an early date. They may not be the same as in modern contracts (which vary considerably around the margins from jurisdiction to jurisdiction) and the details too vary, but the striking factor is the comprehensiveness and similarity with current practice.

Consensus on legal concepts, or, within Greece, fairly standard-ised ways of doing business, does not, however, negate the fact that throughout the period studied, and afterwards during the long period of Roman peace, including it is thought perhaps into the third century CE, the precise Law a particular Greek city complied with was its own. To refer to 'Athens' importing or exporting goods means that either Athenian or its respondent's laws applied. It is the cross-border import-export trade. Athens to Corinth, even on foot, is no real distance (eighty miles, say), but once outside Attica or outside Corinth's territory, different states with independent legal systems existed, so that agreeing terms was not necessarily straightforward. And the complexities of third party interests or wartime restrictions brought into play other legal issues, which might be relevant in particular cases.

There is uncertainty as regards the extent to which in the

ancient world writing or witnessed oral statements were the most common way of confirming an ordinary contractual agreement. But in general it seems likely that, at least in Athens (which has more easily accessible material, and is thus more studied), written recording of governmental activity was common from at least the 6th century BCE. This is likely to have had a 'flowdown' effect on other formal records, such as contracts.

It is important always to keep in mind how relatively complicated it was – at least by comparison with very recent history – to record anything in writing. Even today, when most people in formal business can read and write, contracts are often not put in writing. For small everyday purchases this does not matter, but it is far from unknown for large corporate bodies to find themselves legally pledged in contract unwittingly by unauthorised staff. The embarrassment involved means that this is usually resolved very discreetly.

The other side of the coin, no doubt reflecting the more orally focused societies of the ancients (by comparison with today), is that writing in itself was not seen as the only way to be able to prove an agreement had been made. In practice, it was normal, even when a written record was kept, for the agreement to be witnessed by supporters of both parties. On the contractor's side the witnesses were often also sureties or guarantors for the work to be done, a topic I deal with below. (Given that in our society we do not have a recognised tradition of oral witnesses of contracts, a case could be argued that we are less good at recording contracts than the ancients.)

As regards the retention of written records, Demosthenes, for example, speaking in a court case about a 'private sector' banking loan contract, refers specifically to situations where, for what seemed at the time perfectly reasonable reasons, agreements in writing were destroyed when the contract was discharged. There were conversely occasions where copies of written agreements were entrusted to third parties during execution. Possibly if more had been written down and retained, many of the disputes Demosthenes was involved with would never have come to court; and we would have even less information about everyday practice than we now have. In contract work, however, it is always worth keeping in mind that a written record is no guarantee of an agreed interpretation of an apparent fact.

The paragraphs above cover, primarily from the perspective of legal 'proof', the extent to which a written record of a contract was kept. The epigraphic record retained the 'fair copy' of a contract, but what records would the participants at the time actually have had? Scholars have identified quite a lot. What is instructive is how similar to our present day systems, in so many ways, were the requirements of 'cross border' trade over 2,000 years ago. The carrier – a ship's captain, say – would take with him on his voyage the information required in a convenient format (which at this time might most usually be scratched *ostraka* or strips of soft wood). These would be his 'passport' if he were asked what he was doing on the high seas or elsewhere. Distinction in the contracts was made between what might be needed in times of peace or in times of war, when, as now, the warring parties might well have reasons to monitor or disrupt the trade of the other, and third parties. But of course the actual evidence – the wood strips – have not survived. All we have are references to them.

Those involved in actually carrying out international trade then, as now, probably lived rather differently from the majority of people. Even now, professional sailors live very different lives to those on land and so it was then. Bresson (again in his book *La Cité Marchande*) sums it up rather nicely:

The world of the merchants is a fluid world, fluctuating, a world of interlopers, a world of migratory birds, one day here, tomorrow a hundred different places ... wherever he can find a cargo. The freedom of merchants and their wish to obtain as high a profit as possible, was opposed to the regimentation of the cities ..... the business world is a kind of jungle, a place without rules....'   [*My translation*]

This world is recognisable in the books of Conrad and others of a hundred years ago, in the many small ports tramping ships still call into around the world, including Greece. And, despite hugely increased government regulation, every so often a story comes to light which reminds us that in business, deals are always being done which reflect Bresson's 'jungle', rather than the artificialities of 'official' business. No one in real business wishes to record all that is discussed. It is no wonder that records are scarce.

5

WHAT IS A CONTRACT?

The development of contracting out and 'outsourcing'

In essence, contracting (which really means 'contracting out' or 'outsourcing') happens when those who wish to acquire something or obtain an extra service do not have the means or energy and resolution to do what is needed within their own organisation or 'household'. In ancient Greek, the word *oeconomika* – everything within the direct power of the head of the household – expresses the thought quite well.

When an autocrat rules a people (e.g., in principle in the early empires, or indeed effectively in some states and statelets nowadays) the rulers, by and large, regard those ruled as personal household resources to be used, perhaps as slaves or serfs, to accomplish an activity or service. Of course, autocrats might, and in ancient Greece and elsewhere, often did, 'employ' mercenary soldiers and sailors to fight their wars for them, but this usage, albeit a form of contract, is different conceptually from our idea of a contract because autocracy is, and the decisions autocrats make are, *de facto* above the law.

It is an interesting curiosity that, conceptually, the autocratic tradition is still in force in Britain where the doctrine of Crown Immunity continues to exist. However, in line with pragmatic

British custom, it became accepted that for contractual matters the doctrine was not applied and in due course that practice became enshrined in law, via the Crown Proceedings Act, 1947 and subsequent legislation. This distinction is not needed in most European states, nor in the USA, where the pre-eminence of the Constitution meant that laws had to be passed (e.g., the Tucker Act of 1887) to waive the Federal Government's legal immunities in respect of contractual disputes. Thus we all are obliged, under the rule of law, both the state and its ordinary citizens, to carry out our day-to-day trading businesses subject only to the law and the sanctions of legally binding contracts, actionable in the courts in the event of disagreement. This is in line with the democratic Athenian model.

How does the development of outsourcing under the law come about? It may be worth standing back for a moment and considering. It is probably just capitalistic self-interest in its simplest form. Only when individuals become economically sufficiently well-off to think that they can be independent of reliance on their local autocrat are they in a position to decide for themselves what luxuries (non-essential goods or services) they require. Ideas of what constitutes a luxury change over time and between individuals, but people are only prepared to acquire these items on an as and when required basis – it is a matter of choice. The existence of choice by its very nature is a freedom beyond what an autocrat makes available, which in turn fosters expressions of individualism and provides the incentive for entrepreneurs to make offers via some form of market arrangement. It is then necessary to establish the basis on which transactions are agreed – in other words, the contractual arrangements. In time, only the very poorest in society cannot afford such expressions of individualism.

This process can be observed in the development of contract practice in ancient Greece around the years (very roughly) 550-

500BCE. It may, in part, have been the consequential development of a sense of individual worth and value that spurred some towards the development of a political structure – democracy – where ordinary citizens had a say in politics. However it came about, those newly independent and politicised individuals needed to find ways to value activity on a common basis when transacting the exchange of goods. Money (in Greek τα χρηματα; *ta chremata* – literally 'the things'; 'thingies' in modern English expresses the vagueness of the concept well), became the means. Thus the essentials for contract development – legal certainty and a convenient means of valuation – were in place.

Then came a realisation that greater value could be squeezed from a particular activity if a cheaper means of doing it could be made to work. While slaves may have been relatively cheap, they had to be housed, clothed and fed, and were depreciating assets in the longer term. Specialists, bought in and used as needed, may seem expensive in the context of, for example, day rates, but unlike the individuals of a household, the need to provide for them is limited to the period for which specified work is being done. Maybe such factors, whether overtly understood and expressed or not, contributed to the idea of contracting out in ancient Greece. A Greek view of all these developments, expressed by one much closer in time to it, and therefore with the perspective of his times, was written by the philosopher Aristotle in his important work known as the *Politics*.

This is not the place for a general discussion on economics or what the limits to the growth of outsourcing were in ancient Greece. What is curious, though, is that a similar development pattern for the later part of the scenario, in this case leading to significantly increased levels of contracting out, can be discerned in the history of the large 20th century corporate organisations referred to in Chapter 3. First, as wealth increased, managements gradually accreted more and more resources for internal use – in many ways this was an unconscious reversion to the autocratic model, albeit with the staff benefits (canteens, sports facilities, etc.) the origin of which is Western paternalism.

Then, an underlying cause for the late 20th century move towards contracting out arose because, despite the un-precedented and increasing wealth of post-war society as a whole, proportionally more and more people began to share the economic benefits. The result of this greater sharing was that, in order to continue expansion faster than economic assets themselves could increase, those assets had to be worked much harder than would have been the case in earlier times. The era of asset stripping from the 1970s onward was an early symptom of this effect, but a longer term outcome has been the move to identify and concentrate on 'core business' – as sometimes the only way to survive was to raise capital by selling off 'non-core' business. A consequence was the concomitant need to place under contract more and more essential but 'non-core' activities.

The simplest and first common manifestation of this process within the former huge corporates, nationalised industries and government bodies of the mid-20th century was the replacement of ancillary workers like cleaning or catering staff by contractors, but nowadays there are not many activities where contracted supplies are not purchasable in the marketplace. While undoubtedly pockets of gross inefficiency remain, in the globalised world of early 21st century industry as a whole, there are relatively few large areas where attempts have not been made to reform underused or 'inefficient' resources. Paternalistic amateurism has disappeared and what is called specialism and professionalism is what is expected of business. Contracting out is the norm. Whether this is 'fair' to those who make up the majority of the workforce and whether it is, in the round, an efficient way to run modern society, is a separate matter.

Reverting specifically to ancient Greece, our earliest clear literary source for a contract is from the historian Herodotos. In this mid-6th century BCE deal, the local leaders at Delphi contracted for a leading family clan from Athens – the Alcmaeonids – to rebuild the temple at Delphi (it is uncertain whether this means provide the finance, the materials or the labour, or perhaps all three). There is no reason to regard this contract in itself as exceptional. Herodotos probably only included the reference because the Alcmaeonids received political support from Delphi from doing the job particularly well, and the political result is relevant to his story. The chief point here is that it is an early literary reference to what we would understand as a form of commercial contract.

Most of the surviving epigraphical evidence of contracts is 4th century BCE, but the earliest clear evidence of a commercial contract dates from the end of the 6th century BCE – a contract from Crete for the services of a scribe, Spensithios, dating from around 500BCE. This date is broadly in line with the beginnings of democracies, and therefore the point at which, possibly, there started to be a need or expectation to have an auditable record of a 'public sector' contract; but the survival of the actual epigraph is, in itself, pure chance. There is no reason to suppose this was not just a fairly ordinary, routine contract of its type. From Athens itself, two very short references to elected officials arranging the payment to individuals for work done survive in the records for just after 450BCE. The next paragraphs record a slightly earlier and more significant example.

In general, states always seem to regard self-defence as a 'core' rather than 'non-core' activity. There have always been mercenary soldiers, but only exceptionally do states contract-out core military activities; the risk of losing control to a powerful mercenary general is too great. The extent to which support activities connected with military matters are contracted out is, however, a different matter.

It is therefore interesting that the public accounts of Athens indicate that at least some of the early 5th century BCE wall building at Athens may have been on a day wage basis for hired services. This was a time of national emergency. The Persians, under Xerxes, had invaded Greece, and according to Thucydides the whole population was involved in wall building. While the army's contribution was no doubt 'paid for' as part of the usual cost of maintaining the army, the public accounts are probably reflecting the need to recompense the contribution of those not in the army. However, these payments appear as 'ordinary' contract orders; not, as perhaps could have happened given the emergency situation, as a form of special handouts.

This mixed pattern – the use of internal resources plus small jobbing orders – for defence work at Athens seems to have applied until towards the end of the 5th century. After this there was a long period of what we would call recession. This arose from the downturn in wealth following the devastation and consequent shortage of labour after the Peloponnesian War, a long internecine struggle, 431- 404BCE, between Athens and its allies, and Sparta and its allies, which Athens eventually lost. One result of this was that the internal resources available to Greek cities were severely restricted and that more and more work was contracted out. This outcome was identified as a consequence of a stressed economy over forty years ago by Alison Burford in her book about building developments in Epidaurus 2,500 years ago.[1] The causes she noted are broadly the same in principle as the reasons for the late 20th century changes in our society alluded to above. Whatever the causes in ancient Greece, the 4th century and later evidence that exists suggests that, by these times, contracting for all manner of goods and services was well established and well understood.

---

[1] Burford, A, *The Greek Temple Builders at Epidaurus* (Liverpool, 1969).

There are two fundamental questions (at least) which modern procurement specialists should ask every time a procurement is proposed:
1) Is contracting out the right thing to do in a particular case? Might not a different formulation of the problem result in a solution which is already internally available?
2) If a contractual solution is right, have the customers specified what they want in a way to which the market can recognise and react?

All too often these questions do not get asked and what is purchased is not the optimum solution to the problem. Sometimes, however, having reviewed these questions, it is found that there is no skills base – internal or external – to carry out a particular task. In these cases, clients and suppliers together may need to develop a new and potentially marketable skill.

We have no means of knowing whether and how such questions might have been addressed in antiquity. There are other issues, too, which would certainly be relevant today. For example, could it have been that, however comfortable a city might have been about paying its own workforce in contract to achieve a particular end, they would – all other things being equal – favour known and local contractors rather than itinerants from other states? Such an approach, which at one level is sensible and practical, is still common across the EU nowadays, despite legislation outlawing local preference. Again, we have no means of knowing, as no evidence one way or the other has survived. It is probably extending the question too far to look for further parallels from our day. In the UK we have free economic choice to use, for example, 'Polish plumbers' – or other itinerant labour for agricultural and food production. There is no reason to assume that the Greeks ignored pragmatic factors such as availability, competence and cost. It has been pointed out to me that most of the non-Epidauran contractors for the extensive building works at Epidaurus in the 4th century were from the north-east Peloponnese, a mountainous area without large settlements, so economic migrancy was certainly a factor in construction projects. Of course, such considerations apply only to normal work and ordinary workmen. Although the costs and risks of travelling from city to city and the limitations of ancient transportation would have been relevant, there is no doubt that, as now, the very best people were sought after and recompensed accordingly across the Greek world, regardless of their individual citizen status.

Legal definitions of 'Contract'

Going wider than the Oxford English Dictionary (OED) definition, being 'an agreement between two or more parties enforceable at law', a contract is likely to include a description or specification of what is required and various agreed statements between the parties indicating how they are to achieve the requirement, including clauses setting out the procedures to be used should certain events occur. This is, however, just the aspect of the procurement process which tends to be more legally explicit than other aspects. For this reason, it tends to be the part of the procurement for which records may exist and may therefore survive, albeit that they will only tell some of the story. This is where interpretation of the evidence based upon practical procurement experience may be of value. There is no reason to doubt that the OED definition above aligns broadly with the way the ancient Greeks would have defined 'contract'.

The literary and epigraphical evidence we have makes it clear that they were certain that civilised practices were only practicable if the parties to a contract stuck to the agreement made.

There is a strange apparent conceptual hangover from ancient Greek contracting arrangements which still has modern currency because it expresses a concept essential to the idea of a legal agreement freely entered into by both parties. According to the

Greek author Plutarch, writing 'lives' of ancient Greeks and Romans around 100CE, the Athenian lawgiver Solon (6th century BCE) chose to use the word *seisachtheia*, meaning a 'shaking off of burdens', when trying to find a neutral word to put into his laws; these were aimed, amongst other things, at restarting Athenian society by wiping out the huge debts the poor and landless owed to the rich – the usual problems of extreme inequality which create major changes throughout history. Plutarch has quite a long passage devoted to the discussion of the concept of 'unburdening'. In modern English, this can also be translated as 'discharge'. In English Law, the concept remains that a contract creates burdens or obligations on both parties, and when the burdens come to an end, the phrase still used is that 'the burden of the contract is discharged'. Of course, this serendipitous conjunction of concepts is probably just coincidence, but it is a curious linkage.

The four principles

In modern English practice, the four principles which must be satisfied to create a legally binding contract are often summarised as: 'Offer and Acceptance', 'Intention', 'Capacity' and 'Consideration'. Do the equivalents of these concepts appear in ancient Greek practices? I believe that they do. The commentary following is written strictly from the perspective of a present day practitioner of procurement, and I deliberately do not go into precise detail regarding exact legal definitions and distinctions, as they do not affect 99.99% of contracts.

Principle 1 – Offer and Acceptance (including evidence of what has been done – Transparency)

This encompasses the legal concept that two parties freely reach agreement through a negotiation process. The parties may do this either informally OR there may be a much more formal arrangement – e.g., a tender process, whereby a client organisation may elect to invite more than one supplier to bid for a proposed job, in which case a rigorous 'competitive tender' may be issued inviting proposals or tenders on an equal basis, facilitating ease of comparison of those tenders once received. Once an offer has been accepted, neither party can unilaterally change the legal agreement (which is not to say that this doesn't happen intentionally or unintentionally all the time). In recent years in the UK, there has been a much greater emphasis, especially but not exclusively in the public sector, on the need for transparency of process in the interests of fairness and for audit.

All these modern criteria were identified and catered for in Greek practice. The ancient Greek processes for creating and validating a legal agreement were studied many years ago,[1] and it is well established that, in principle, they differ little from those still used. As indicated above, and as is the case now, a written agreement is not essential for a binding contract to exist, albeit that the practical problems of providing evidence that a oral contract is enforceable means that it would be unwise not to provide the certainty of an objective mechanism.

There is a record that the lawgiver Solon ordered that the parties to a contract should swear an oath (i.e. get the gods to witness/ put the deed on the god's honour) if no witnesses were present. It looks as if Solon attempted to allow a form of independent certainty for the parties, even if no other record was practicable. Maybe compliance was encouraged by the fact that, in ancient Greek oath practice, a curse was often called down upon those who did not fulfil the promises made.

I touched on written contract records above. Even after writing down what was agreed became a normal way of recording agreements, the ancient Greeks continued to use the witness

---

[1] e.g., Pringsheim, F, *Greek Law of Sale* (Weimar, 1950). Although out of date, this is still a useful starting point for studies in this area.

system and to record (in writing) which citizens were witnesses to each contract. The witness system no doubt arose before writing was widespread, but what is interesting is that it continued to be used. This may reflect two main points – first, as is usual in society, a conservative attitude to change for change's sake, but second, the deep seated preference the ancient Greeks always showed for transparency as regards what (in the case of 'public sector' contracts at least) their elected representatives were doing on their behalf. For an example of how important witnesses were for an ancient Greek contract see the photograph and translation of a typical contract in the Appendix.

This feature of Greek public governance – the creation of a transparent record of what was agreed – was emphasised by Aristotle, who identified audit and accountability by the whole body of citizens as a feature of Athenian democracy. The epigraphical records of contracts kept in public places were a means of informing the citizen body of what had been agreed on their behalf (and also, no doubt, as a convenient way for the parties to confirm what they had agreed). Since similar evidence also exists from city states which did not follow the Athenian democratic model, it seems reasonable to conclude that the same reasoning applied in these states also. Those who ruled non-democratic states might well have found it useful to publicise at least those aspects of what had been done that reflected well on them. Either way, this led to the need to record activities and, where applicable, contracts.

An interesting gloss is put on the issue of witnesses by Theophrastos, who lived around 300BCE. He noted that, for house purchase contracts, the little city of Thurium had a special arrangement. The parties paid a small sum of money to the three nearest neighbours to ask them to act as witnesses to the prospective deal. From a modern property perspective this is an interesting angle as it goes against our ways of doing things.

Modern contracts specialists will note in this regard that interested third parties and the payment of consideration were involved – an early example of the application of the philosophy contained in our modern UK Contracts (Rights of Third Parties) Act 1999, which legal advisers frequently insist is explicitly excluded from effect in contracts. Furthermore, the practice explicitly gave transparency about who was buying and selling, which must have affected behaviours (property developers and gazumpers take note). But I digress.

By the 4th century BCE a written document, filed away for later reference, was often the preferred way of establishing what had been agreed. Demosthenes, for example, in the context of a speech mainly about a banking loan for overseas trade contracting, said that:

> For whereas clauses in contract subject to dispute require a judicial decision .... those, on the contrary, which are admitted to by both the contracting parties, and about which there exist written agreements, are held by all men to be final; and the parties are bound to abide by what is written.

As the speech is about a wholly private sector contract, not one in which public sector issues were involved, this reference tends to reinforce the point that, by Demosthenes' time (mid-4th century BCE), written records of contracts were already being used in much the same way as we use them nowadays. Unlike ancient Greek practice, in modern times private and public sector contracts in the UK and Europe-wide were, in general, not available for scrutiny except by the few formal audit bodies set up to monitor them. Thirty years ago, one of the attractions of being involved within procurement type commerce was that, apart from contract law itself, large swathes of what could be done were effectively unregulated. Inevitably therefore, even in the public sector, only the most significant or outrageous audit queries were followed up, and the amount of press and popular knowledge of contracting was very limited.

Today this has changed in some respects. It has largely been the pressure for transparency from European institutions which led, with full effect following the 1988 Single European Act, to a resurgence of interest in the transparency and audit of contracts. There is now a huge EC Directives compliance industry, covering public sector contracting and even (as a consequence of public sector sub-contract transparency) some aspects of private sector contracting.

The Freedom of Information Act 2000 has also had some effect, though by no means as much as many public sector organisations expected when it came into force. In some ways, the wheel has turned full circle. In principle, EU citizens may now, if they wish, fairly easily track down and scrutinise information about contracts generally, and public sector contracts in particular. However, sight of the actual contract documents is likely to be refused on grounds of 'commercial confidentiality'. It still falls short of the level of transparency that was given by the ancient practice of writing the terms of the contract on stone in the market place, but recent proposals by the UK coalition government in 2010 may mean that we are approaching that level of transparency again.

An interesting modern gloss on transparency occurred in the 1990s after the European Community had revised their public procurement regulations so as to make them more stringent. Bidders for work were given the right to challenge decisions made by public sector buying organisations if they believed that the buying organisation had not applied the regulations accurately when offering contracts in the market place. (Usually the challenger was a competing firm which had seen the work go elsewhere.) The EU included in the regulations an 'Attestation' (witness) mechanism whereby buying organisations could, if they wished, engage approved third party bodies to attest (i.e.

witness) that the rules had been properly followed. To the best of the author's knowledge, this scheme was only ever tried out in Eire and it did not catch on.

A broadly similar revitalisation of this witness concept, though not one that is explicitly about transparency, has been the move towards the use of independent Adjudicators (independent third parties who have the right to read and interpret contract details) in the event of disputes. The law requires this for all building and civil engineering contracts in the UK. It is also a requirement in contracts undertaken under the standard conditions of contracts known as the NEC (which originally stood for 'New Engineering Contract' but today has been re-branded simply as NEC) published by the UK Institution of Civil Engineers. NEC is today used worldwide.

Principle 2 – Intention

This is about the parties being able to demonstrate that they intended to make a legally binding agreement. As discussed in Chapter 4, the Greeks recorded their contractual intentions, initially by involving witnesses and later by written documentation. One speech by Demosthenes preserves the actual wording of the clause setting out their precise contractual intentions:

And in regard to these matters [above] nothing shall have greater effect than the agreement.

Principle 3 – Capacity

I have found two simple literary references to Capacity. Theophrastos wrote:

[house purchase] contracts must be made from one who is not drunk, not acting from anger or contentiousness, not of unsound mind, but mentally competent and (in general) acting lawfully.

WHAT IS A CONTRACT?

Plutarch says that the lawgiver Solon prescribed that:

> [a will made] .... under the influence of sickness or drugs or imprisonment or extorted by compulsion or by the pressure exerted by a wife, was not enforceable.

Arrangements about personal wills are not the same as commercial contracts but the criteria are similar – and, as procurement professionals know, both quotations above use virtually the same words as modern wording which covers the same point.

The idea that one must be of sound mind before engaging in legal affairs may perhaps just be regarded as common sense. It does, of course, depend upon what true sound mind is. An example of this point in action in the ancient Greek world is in the record of the speech 'Against Athenogenes'. The speechwriter Hyperides wrote it to try to rescue the unnamed speaker from the contractual consequences of his own actions. (Individuals usually had to present their case to the courts in person, but it was fully in order for them to pay a speechwriter to prepare what they were going to say, leaving them just to learn or read it. It is conventional to refer to the speechwriters as the 'orators'. Sometimes they were themselves politicians. Of these, Demosthenes is the best known.)

The case raises all manner of issues which are debated, but the relevant point here is a single one which I have not found mentioned in this way in any commentaries on the speech: the speaker had failed to do full due diligence before committing to a purchase. His opponent, Athenogenes, would have ruined him if he could not persuade the jury to allow him to put the contract aside. The speaker admits to carelessness, inexperience of the implications of legal agreements and the reason-sapping effects of passionate love, as justifications for bad decision making. (This is the 'crime passionelle' defence with which we are still familiar – all embracing passion deflects people from making judgements in fully sound mind.) The law in principle was clear then, as it is now: in contract, the doctrine of *caveat emptor* applies, and it was that principle that the speech was attempting to mitigate. Just as today, judicial decisions in particular cases depended upon individual issues and the skills of the advocate.

Examples from literature indirectly emphasise the point that, in ancient Greece, the right to buy and sell in a city state was a normal personal right deriving from citizenship. Thucydides, for example, explicitly mentions that the Spartan government, in stripping the rights of citizenship from the Spartans who were captured in a military disaster, deprived them of their right to buy and sell. By contrast, the philosopher Plato, discussing the rights needed by the leaders of his ideal state, does not see a use for these rights on the grounds that they are practical skills needed for practical men, rather than the pure skills needed for leaders. Plato's view of the pure (academic) skills for leadership, over the practical skills of industry or commerce, have lived on and influenced Western thought patterns down through the centuries. Perhaps modern procurement professionals, as they argue their case (often unsuccessfully) that organisations should view procurement strategically rather than tactically, should blame Plato for their predicament.

Principle 4 – Consideration

In English Law 'consideration' (a good legal definition is 'some right, interest, profit or benefit accruing to one party; or some forbearance, detriment, loss or responsibility given, suffered, or undertaken by the other'; Lush, J, quoted in *Anson's Law of Contract*[1]) is necessary for the formation of every legally enforceable simple contract. Slightly different definitions apply

---

[1] Guest (Ed.), in *Anson's Law of Contract*, 21st Edition (Oxford, 1959).

outside English law (e.g., in the United States) and English contracts under seal do not require consideration.

I have not managed to identify any ancient Greek commentary on contract-specific evidence of consideration – or the *quid pro quo* principle in practice. I do observe, however, that all the ancient Greek contracts that I tracked down (and there are over 150 substantial ones) include somewhere in the wording a reference to payment being made in exchange for work. There is also some broadly analogous evidence, the best being from Herodotos who, commenting on the Lydian/Median marriage contract between Alyattes and Astyages, wrote, 'In the absence of consideration, agreements won't be kept'; or, an alternative translation:'treaties seldom remain intact without powerful sanctions.'

Although the example relates to a marriage contract (and, admittedly, a non-Greek one), Herodotos' comment seems to be a general one about human nature, and may perhaps be extended to include routine commercial practice. The significant point, however, is that general principle: an incentive, such as money, is needed to make the parties comply with a contract.

The lawgiver Solon (again according to Plutarch) recognised in his laws that, except under compulsion, no one does something for nothing (I paraphrase). And if it was that spirit which encouraged the development of civic and commercial life in Athens, it might not be stretching the argument too far to see an example of a quasi-contractual relationship between the citizen and the state being recognised by consideration. Demosthenes has a defendant say, when summoned to appear in court:

I deposited a drachma (in Court) against the charge to me as proof that I hadn't failed to appear as the law requires.

Regardless of the specifics, the very normality we assume in this statement as regards making a payment for a service emphasises its overall significance. Our lives, whether or not we are conscious of it, are to a large extent governed by the norms of contractual relationships, and these modern relationships are similar to ancient Greek practice.

6

TYPES OF PROCUREMENT TRANSACTION

In my study of the content of classical Greek contracts I have come across examples of the use of nearly all the types of procurement transaction in the ancient record that are known to me as a modern practitioner. The things that people buy may change over time, as does the way they are packaged, but the basic categorisation of supplies, building works, technical manufacture (e.g., devise and make a new shield) and services – e.g., practical, such as water engineering or plumbing, and intellectual, such as the services of a speech writer, which we might now call public relations, spin doctoring or legal consultancy – all existed in principle. So, too, did the trade-off between purchase versus lease, which is essentially long-term hire on special terms, as opposed to short-term hire/borrowing.

However, in terms of number and volume, it would seem likely that most ancient procurement contracts were, as today, to do with the provision of straightforward goods or services. Some of the most significant (albeit scanty) records come from the building trade, no doubt because these were most often public/private contracts and therefore there was a need for a public record to be kept. There are, for example, accounting records on stone of payments for some hundreds of very simple building contracts, or orders. However we find no conditions recorded (beyond the implicit assumption that work must be done so that payment can be made). A recent study[1] of work undertaken by named individual workmen according to surviving publicly recorded accounts at Athens, Epidaurus, Delphi and Delos, has analysed this kind of order, and information on how the work might have been organised. The most simple may take the form, e.g., 'x to supply wood, dimensions abc, for price z', etc., but some involve skilled tasks, e.g., 'x to cut an architrave for price y', etc., and others, which provide for fees or stipends to, e.g., secretaries, are simple contracts for employment. In principle, these are contracts let on what we now call the 'traditional' system – the client takes responsibility for all the work, calling in supplies and minor suppliers as necessary, and by the same token is responsible if something goes wrong outside the immediate remit of the contractor – if, for example, the architrave cut to the specified dimensions does not fit with the masonry blocks next to it, also cut to the right dimensions, etc., but by another contractor.

These orders are important in themselves as evidence which has survived of 'day to day' ancient Greek commerce, but in procurement terms there are other types of much more interesting contract for which, fortunately, we also have evidence. Some indeed are complex contracts, with quite detailed specifications and conditions. Two of the most informative are Athenian – that of the Prostoon and that of the Arsenal at Athens.

The surviving Prostoon (or Portico) inscription is unfortunately deficient as a contract, but it does contain a fairly full specification for the work. What is interesting about it is that the surviving text contains an example of Embodiment Loan. This concept is still

---

[1] Feyel, C, *Les artisans dans les sanctuaires grecs aux époques classique et hellénistique á travers la documentation financière en Grec* (De Boccard, 2006).

useful today, and its use in this 4th century BCE contract simply emphasises how similar practical contract administration today is by comparison with then. In this contract, the client – the State – provided separately for the contractor, free of charge, the lead and iron for connecting the stones, and a pulley for him to use.

The Arsenal Contract is one of the most complete of all the inscriptions that have survived. It gives a clear working specification for the building work – which must be in accordance with the contract, the measurements and model supplied (clearly no diagrams) – with references to the need for the contractor to comply with the architect's instructions and the agreed delivery dates. The use of a model is interesting; we still use models when appropriate, although mostly nowadays we rely on textual descriptions and diagrams. But the use of models as specifications from which contractors can work is well attested in more recent historical times; the cathedral builders used them for example, as regularly did the British Admiralty over at least the last 400 years, and civil and mechanical engineers and others still do to illustrate points in the detailed specification.

From experience I know that there are today in the UK thousands of much less well drafted specifications than the Arsenal one, creating technical uncertainty and commercial havoc every day of the week. Given the costs and effort of inscription writing, and evidence from other contracts (which specify that the contractor publishes, on stone, and at his expense, the agreed terms of contract) it is probable that the Arsenal inscription we have is, in fact, the real working document to which the parties originally agreed. Contractual transparency in action!

The other major source of information about ancient goods and services contracts, and the only area where there is much evidence of what we would today call private sector commerce, is from the import/export business. Unlike the public/private sector, such records as we have are not epigraphical; rather they are literary and from the courtrooms where such meagre records as have survived are frequently about import/export and shipping disputes. It is only an impression, but my perception is that courtroom disputes over this category of contract, followed probably by those about building work, remain the most frequent kind of contractual dispute. The tradition of Demosthenes and his near contemporaries in this area is still very much alive at the modern commercial courts, and this happens partly because import/export is the area where domestic and non-domestic practices may most often come up against each other, but also because so many contracts continue to be drafted in such a way that one party or another can see an opportunity to gain as a result of lack of clarity in the contract provisions.

Another area of ancient Greek contracting which, relative to other types of contract, features to a greater extent than may be expected, is property lease contracting. Property contracts generally are a commercial area (like banking) that does not feature large in the careers of most procurement professionals. There are good reasons for the prominence in the Greek record of this kind of contract. As is the case nowadays, a property lease tends to be in force for a period of years rather than the short periodicity of a typical contract for goods or services. Leases then, as now, were associated with significant expenditure, committed over a period of years. Relatively speaking, large numbers of people were involved – probably because what we would now regard as public sector organisations were obliged to demonstrate public accountability transparency and open records. In ancient Greece, lease agreements appear usually to have been recorded on stone and the stone placed in a public place. These stones were called ὅροι (*horoi*). Often the lease was between phratries (associations/ civic sub-divisions with mutual backgrounds/interests) or 'town councils', and individuals (and their families). Many are for the maintenance of shrines and their surrounding areas.

In modern terms the practice can be roughly compared to, say, a council or other public body, putting a notice in the local newspaper about their intentions and then having to keep available, in the public records office, the detailed register of their agreement. Modern day 'commercial confidentiality' means that this comparison does not quite work, but the analogy is not too far removed from the ancient Greek reality. The terms were recorded in a fairly set way on the *horos* stone at the entrance to the property. While all such evidence is extremely useful in trying to build up a knowledge of ancient Greek business, and I have used evidence from the detailed clauses of these agreements as examples when applicable, it would be misleading to consider property leases as being typical of ordinary purchase and sale contracts.

No doubt it is as a consequence of a body of evidence being to hand that there have been a number of studies of ancient Greek leasing. They have shown that leasing, especially in Athens and areas particularly exposed to Athenian ways, was a common way to do business since there was a civic need to organise and maintain public areas – e.g., shrines to the gods, or to obtain an income for the use of municipal land. It also involved large amounts of cash which meant that the financial system had to be large enough to cope. However, there is much less evidence for private property leasing, perhaps because, without a need to write down publicly what had been agreed, the chances of a record surviving are minimal.

There is, however, another aspect of what I class as 'leasing' contracts that may be of interest to the modern practitioner. These are contracts relating to the maintenance of, for example, temple grounds, including sometimes the building of structures, or the maintenance of services on public land. These were usually relatively long-term and sometimes involved significant sums of money. These ancient contracts share features with that much disputed modern innovation in contracting – the UK government's

Public Finance Initiative (PFI) or Public Private Partnership (PPP) arrangements. Unfortunately (as it could be an attractive idea) I doubt that PFI/PPPs in themselves demonstrate features such that there are enough especial similarities between the ancient Greek lease contract and a PPP contract to make treating this type of contract worthy of consideration over and above the more general points of contract comparison I have made in respect of contracts generally. I make further comments linked to this idea in the last Chapter.

Finally, there are also ancient Greek records of property purchase – sale contracts, and, just for completeness, examples of the 'mortgage' arrangements themselves. Property purchase – sale contracts appear to have taken a very simple and straightforward form, and as they are not 'procurements' in the usual sense of the term used in commerce, I do not propose to discuss them further. Also, 'mortgage' arrangements in the *horoi* inscriptions are by my definition more akin to banking and finance matters than commercial contracting.

7

PROCUREMENT STRATEGIES AND CONTRACT MANAGEMENT

Once the 'make or buy' decision has been made in favour of 'buy', it is essential that the most suitable procurement strategy to satisfy the activity being contemplated is devised. However, if the strategy is not followed through by effective and pragmatic Contract Management, the final result may prove to be a disappointment. There are literally hundreds of books and articles on these topics, some of which may be worth reading.

An important point, not often observed, is that every procurement decision should go through the same basic process, regardless of value or complexity. The reason due process is not always engaged is that those not trained in procurement processes often find it difficult to accept that the thinking process behind a minor revenue purchase is, in principle, the same as that required for a major capital project. Obviously a decision to buy some stationery, a few nails, or an electric heater, is of small financial importance to most organisations, so less time and effort needs to be invested in undertaking procurement activity than, for example, a major capital investment. The problem comes however if there are lots of people all over an organisation who have some peripheral involvement in procurement decisions but who have no immediate interest in seeing the wider purchasing issues and opportunities. All too often this leads to different departments and disciplines purchasing inefficiently. Money is wasted and supply risk increases – even for minor purchases. Hence I make no apology for suggesting that the basic decision structure properly employed to carry out a major procurement should be applied to develop suitable strategies for purchases of every type and value including where relevant, an associated Contract Management plan.

In 2007, the UK Chartered Institute of Purchasing and Supply (CIPS) in its role as the leading professional organisation for procurement, published a guide on the subject.[1] In brief, it said that Contract Management is regarded as successful if:

a) the arrangements for service delivery continue to be satisfactory to both parties

b) the expected business benefits and value for money are being achieved

c) the supplier is co-operative and responsive

d) the organisation understands its obligations under the contract

e) there are no disputes

f) there are no surprises

g) efficiencies are being realised

It continued:

The foundations for effective and successful post-award contract management rely upon careful, comprehensive and thorough implementation of the upstream or pre-award activities. During

---

[9] *Contract Management Guide* – CIPS (published on www.cips.org.uk in 2007).

the pre-award stages, the emphasis should be focused on why the contract is being established and on whether the supplier will be able to deliver in service and technical terms. However, careful consideration must be given to how the contract will work once it has been awarded. The organisation's high-level requirements should be carefully researched so that there is clarity of purpose from the outset. This will help to ensure clarity in all aspects of the procurement process. Management of contracts, particularly partnerships, requires flexibility on both sides and a willingness to adapt the terms of the contract to reflect changing circumstances. It is important to recognise that problems are bound to arise which could not be foreseen when the contract was awarded. Activities involved include:

Upstream or pre-award activities such as:

a) preparing the business case and securing management approval;
b) assembling the project team
c) developing contract strategy
d) risk assessment
e) developing contract exit strategy
f) developing a contract management plan
g) drafting specifications and requirements
h) establishing the form of contract
i) establishing the pre-qualification, qualification and tendering procedures
j) appraising suppliers
k) drafting Invitation to Tender documents
l) evaluating tenders
m) negotiation
n) awarding the contract

Downstream or post-award activities:

o) changes within the contract

p) service delivery management

q) relationship management

r) contract administration

s) assessment of risk

t) purchasing organisation's performance and effectiveness review

u) contract closure

That such documents are still needed reflects the reality that delivering a contract satisfactorily and achieving the objectives required under the terms of the contract is in practice very difficult. This is why, in the end, it is how people work together – regardless of the formal position – that constitutes success or failure to those involved, either as participants or as recipients (customers). If it works well, and more importantly if the outcome is well regarded, only specialists take an interest in the process, whether the contract was delivered on time or under or over budget, etc. If there are problems, everyone becomes interested, and for a period all manner of people appear to have a view on the matter – until the world moves on.

As time is the great healer, no one now knows or (except perhaps a few specialists) cares whether the Parthenon was built to the original budget and in the specified time. The same point applies to most great monuments, such as our cathedrals, and this will probably apply, too, to more recent British horror projects such as the Scottish Parliament or the Millennium Bridge. From this perspective, what can be said about ancient Greek contracting processes, using, very broadly, the headings set out above as a way of identifying the issues?

Preparing the business case and securing management approval

Organisations have all manner of different ways to raise money and allocate risk, and no doubt it was always so. We are now unlikely ever to come across the records of, say, the meetings of the Athenian assembly which authorised the building of parts of the Acropolis, though we know from the epigraphical record that (as we might expect, given our knowledge of the Athenian constitution) management boards were appointed annually to supervise the individual building works.

One small piece of evidence we do have is Plutarch's commentary in his *Pericles* which contends that, shortly after the middle of the 5th century BCE, the Athenian statesman Pericles persuaded the Athenians to construct the Acropolis buildings we know today. It was a redevelopment project – the Parthenon we know is at least the third building on the site – and it involved much more extensive and expensive work than many Athenians thought was necessary. Plutarch's evidence may not be reliable. His interest was not in Pericles' project management prowess and he was writing more than 600 years later. Contractually, from the limited and incidental evidence we have from the accounting records that have survived, it looks as if the project was a mixture – mostly what we now regard as 'traditional' client-led piecemeal contracting, but with some work fully outsourced to specialists. Unfortunately, although we all know that the redevelopment of the Acropolis was completed, whether the outcome was regarded at the time as a successfully managed project is beyond our capacity to know.

The distinction between the detailed client control of 'traditional' project contracting and contractor-led outsourced techniques, especially when huge sums of money and resources are involved, and particularly when government deadlines and credibility are at stake, is rarely fully maintained in practice.

Recent UK projects where a conflict between meeting a deadline, prestige, and cost control became problematic are the London Millennium Dome and the Scottish Parliament building. What we do know of the Acropolis project suggests that from at least as early as the mid-5th century, when Pericles made his case to the Athenian Assembly, those anxious for work to be done understood the need to plan a strategy and secure as much support from potential interested parties as they could. It is a reasonable supposition, based on experience of what usually happens, that there were those who were not persuaded of the need for the particular project or who had 'axes to grind' and did what they could to embarrass or complicate the lives of those trying to drive through the project. Modern project managers and others will recognise the scenario well.

At the start of any project involving a significant procurement element, the buying organisation's management group should make (among other project due diligence activities) a rigorous assessment of the real scope that the buying organisation will have, once contracts are let, to control in practice the contracts on a day-to-day basis. This is determined by a range of factors including internal expertise, the relative bargaining strengths of the parties, technical complexity, the competitiveness of the particular market, and the specific terms and conditions of contract that are to be used. The issue is fundamentally about power in the marketplace on the general commercial principle that it is likely that the party with the bigger commercial clout determines the legal and commercial arrangements. It is essential to understand the dynamics of the relevant market sector to judge this correctly, and this is not always obvious. Patterns of supply and demand fluctuate. Although there are always special cases (e.g., monopoly supply; unique personal skills, etc.) this does not deflect from the principle that, if the procurement is done properly, buyer's terms should normally prevail. The evidence suggests that

2,500 years ago the Greeks were as aware of this as anyone is nowadays. One possible way of pre-empting negotiations in this area is for contracting organisations to set up long-term contract arrangements to agreed terms and conditions and then just 'call off' supplies, etc., when they are needed. If both parties intend to have long-term contractual relations, this helps smooth out short-term fluctuations. A contractual inscription, which may be the evidence needed to show how the Greeks attempted to cover this issue in their public sector contracting, is discussed below.[1]

Ideally, the business case phase provides the opportunity to clarify to colleagues in one's own organisation what one wants to buy and when it must be bought. Timing is critical, since unless one can approach the market from a position of strength, with the option to walk away or delay, potential suppliers will sense that they, rather than the buyer, can more easily dictate the terms. It seems likely, for example, that the global commercial market will determine the terms on which the British Government (ultimately) will have to ensure that there is sufficient new energy generation in future years. The market is likely to give less favourable deals than would have been the case were there not an urgent need to overcome the UK energy shortages forecast within the next few years (2012 – 2022).

Once the contract is let there are even more constraints on the buyer. As mentioned above, the need to complete the Millennium Dome project for 1st January, 2000 meant that those trades on the project's critical path (e.g., electricians) were able to sell their services at a premium. At the time of writing it seems as if the procurements for the London Olympics in 2012 may avoid these problems, but the 2010 Delhi Commonwealth Games procurement was a well publicised and very different story. No

---

[1] See discussion of Tegea, in Chapter 9.

doubt the relevant BP buyers' priorities after the 2010 Louisiana oil spill were for immediate expertise and equipment, irrespective of the short-term cost.

The ancient Greeks had similar difficulties. Their perennial problem, and one that has not troubled western Europe for some years now, was food supply. Ensuring that the city states had sufficient supplies of grain to feed their urban populations was always a concern, and malnutrition, if not starvation of the weakest, was an ever present worry except when there were good harvests. By the 4th century the epigraphical evidence is clear that when food shortages occurred, city states were often at the mercy of those who had grain to sell.

Studies by scholars on trade and economics discuss these issues from those perspectives. A number of Demosthenes' political and private orations are about particular grain crises at Athens and elsewhere. In these circumstances the supplier has the whip hand, and so it was in ancient Greece. Often those who came to the aid of the state in its hour of need did well financially and, perhaps more importantly given the customs and culture of the times, received public recognition, such as a formal civic reception, seats at the front of the theatre, etc. They might also receive relief from taxes for many years. Inevitably these benefits gave the supplier extra influence and power over the state's policies. Since a number of these 'saviours of the state' were not citizens but outsiders (metics), in practice what happened was that sometimes non-citizens ended up with greater powers than the citizens themselves. Maybe some would say that not entirely dissimilar benefits can be the reward non-domiciled status offers in modern states.

Since raising, accounting for, and spending money are all issues which have to be addressed by those responsible for authorising contracts, I will deal with this next.

8

EXCURSUS — FINANCIAL ISSUES

Business Risk and Personal Liability

In ancient and pre-industrial society business tended to be small scale – e.g., one man or family, albeit perhaps a rich and powerful family (though the wealth of the 5th century BCE Athenians would have been but small change to the fabled wealth of the 1st century BCE Crassus of Rome). This affects how business risk is perceived; if an individual lost control and the business went down, so did the individual and his family. Unfortunately, throughout history there have been, and will continue to be, outcomes of this kind.

One way of spreading risk and increasing capital available is for bands of individuals to contract as a group. This practice, still current today in the form of partnerships, was common in antiquity. We have plenty of evidence of special interest societies in ancient Greece, often based on phratries (associations/civic sub divisions) together contracting out land and property to be serviced and maintained on their behalf by an individual or group of individuals. In the event of difficulties, in principle, as today, each individual was responsible for their liability. Such mechanisms spread risk but still leave it with individuals.

Another approach was for a third party, or parties, to act as the contractor's surety or guarantor. From both the literary and epigraphical evidence we have, it is clear that this route was very widely used in ancient Greece, both when the parties were individuals but also when a number of people were involved. It is not usually explicitly spelt out in the contract record exactly what those responsibilities are, suggesting that the practice was so commonplace (perhaps a long-standing legislative requirement) that there was no need. Fortunately, we have evidence from Demosthenes, and especially inscriptions (see next paragraphs) which do provide us with some information. In many ways the guarantor role (whether one person or many) is equivalent to taking out insurance. No evidence of such sureties have been found for simple orders so it seems this was a practice reserved for more complex transactions, which suggests that what we would today call a risk assessment was undertaken. In recent years doing formal risk assessments has become normal best practice, and if the risk is seen to be worth laying off to a third party, the usual route is to seek either a parent company or a banker's guarantee.

A feature of surviving Greek contracts and leases is the frequency of the references to the names of those standing surety to the contractor for the completion of the contracted work, and, where text survives, the evidence is that the sureties would be obliged to make restitution to the client. Where there are no such references in significant contracts, the more likely reason is that the text is defective rather than that guarantors did not exist. So it is probably correct to say that, normally, significant contracts were explicitly backed by surety arrangements. It could even be argued that this system gave the Greek client more financial certainty than his equivalent today. A particular example which makes the point especially well – if the text (which is not entirely clear) has been correctly interpreted – is a 5th century lead tablet from near Perpignan which seems to be essentially a personal aide memoire for one of the parties to a contract. It looks as if this transaction involved half the money on account, followed by the second half on delivery, and that there were two separate sets of guarantors, one for each transaction.

Research is still being done to try to understand more about those prepared to act as guarantors. On the basis that no one would be prepared to act as a guarantor (or be accepted) unless they had the means to contribute to the guarantee if needed, it makes sense to assume that the guarantor must have had some interest in the matter or surplus wealth that they wished to use. Thus it is not a surprise that sometimes the guarantors for contracts were the same people as those who commissioned the work. Perhaps more generally it was a practice of the rich to put their wealth to use, and at risk, as guarantors. There is also evidence that fellow contractors could be guarantors for someone in the same line of business. Commercially, this practice would seem very sensible, provided it did not lead to an over restricted number of guarantors affected by the same problem (so that if a number defaulted, everyone would be out of business). Given the potential for losing money if things went wrong, there must have been some benefit for taking on this role. The evidence is currently tenuous. Perhaps a fee or a percentage applied, or where public works were concerned it might have been tax relief (*ateleia*) or public recognition for good citizenship. There is quite a lot of evidence for such recognition to public benefactors, but none link specifically to the role that a guarantor of a contract may have played.

Accepting individual risk continued for centuries. It was only when industrialisation and population growth in the nineteenth century totally changed the scale of organisations and the need for capital to finance expansion, so that no single individual or select small group of individuals were likely to be the sole owners, that changes were made to the liability regime. The 1862 Corporation Act brought into English law the fully developed concept that one's individual risk could be limited through the creation of a corporate entity. This idea had been developing across the world, especially in the US, UK, France and Germany, in the first half of the 19th century.

Whereas the existence of the corporate entity has undoubtedly facilitated the accumulation of capital and creation of global organisations, the *quid pro quo* has been a common assumption that the checks and balance of corporate life would mitigate against unduly risky individual business decision making. The 2008/9 banking crisis, however, suggests that in certain circumstances a failing corporate governance structure can lead to greater risks to society as a whole than could ever have been encountered through reckless individual entrepreneurial risk taking. The massive shared and globalised risk in intangible financial "products" was never anticipated when the legal concept of limited liability was developed. In Rome very large scale capital acquisition was possible, financed by the long-term expansion of the Empire, so maybe a comparison of aspects of the 2008-9 banking crisis with the many financial crises that wracked the Roman world as it ceased to expand rapidly could be instructive. This, of course, is far beyond the scope of this book.

The ancient Greeks always recognised that sea travel was potentially dangerous. The risks of storms, shipwreck, piracy, accidents, etc., when trading across the Mediterranean, were substantial. Relatively large sums of money were needed to buy or hire a ship and/or to be able to buy a cargo with which to trade. This led to the development of bottomry (a form of maritime insurance) whereby the idea of a financial guarantor for a venture evolved such that specialist guarantors (we would call them brokers) were prepared to underwrite the risks in the hope of the massive profits possible from a succcessful voyage. The result of this was that shipowners often went to sea owing large sums to the bank – which was fine if they had a profitable voyage, but potential penury if not. If they went down with the ship their own problems might be solved, but it might not be so simple for their heirs or for those who had put up the money. This was a source of business for courtroom speechwriters like Demosthenes. For a fairly recent analogy, one has only to remember the problems of the Lloyd's 'names' in the 1980s.

In the 21st century there are still very many 'family firms' that, although protecting individual liability via limited company status and liability insurances, effectively risk the family future on the success of their business ventures. It is, therefore, perhaps feasible to hold that, in principle, there is ultimately little difference between the way a modern businessman and a Greek over 2,000 years ago would have addressed financial risk assessment. The facilities and techniques now available to mitigate disaster are potentially more diverse – but possibly no more effective in the end. The scale of options for trade in the modern world is infinitely greater than was available then. But typically many small firms are either unable or unwilling to consider risks objectively, so they do not benefit from the risk mitigation options available to large corporations. In principle, it is personal circumstance and motivation that remain the criteria as to the extent to which any particular individual is prepared to take on business risk to facilitate a lifestyle choice.

Ways of financing transactions

If one has capital, the capital can be invested by carrying out a commercial transaction, ideally at a profit. If one does not have capital, but needs to trade to live, the problem is then a calculation as to how best to fund the transaction. As the ancient Greeks appear to have developed the use of money as a fiduciary concept, they had the wherewithal to be able to do business in ways very similar to us nowadays. Research published in recent years on ancient Greek banking practices has shown how sophisticated the system was, with plenty of sources of credit supply for entrepreneurs. By the 4th century the credit market was so well established and the banking system so reliable that gradually some banks developed specialisations in particular aspects of banking activity. A significant number of the banks were the sanctuaries and shrines of the gods (see next paragraph), and what we would now call market consolidation happened. Small private bankers could not compete with the largest sanctuaries, e.g., that of Delos, so the market became less generally open to all and the largest 'sanctuary-banks' became even richer.

It was the practice of the ancient Greeks, when e.g., they won a victory in battle, to dedicate some of the spoils to one of the sanctuaries of the gods as tribute gifts. These were then usually carefully recorded (and published) so that visitors could see where the wealth had come from. The most famous sanctuaries in what we now know as Greece were Olympia, Delos, Delphi and Athens. By the end of the 5th century (to take a particular time when, as shown above, commerce had substantially developed) each had become rich and it appears that it became a practice for surplus unspent wealth from the spoils (a fiduciary concept indeed) to be used to finance the building of better temples, etc. The bullion and valuable articles in the sanctuaries would either have been sold off, or used as collateral for other borrowing – hence a form of banking.

Athens in particular had become very rich during the 5th century, and the wealth in the Parthenon, Athene's Acropolis temple, was used to finance the cost of redeveloping the Acropolis into the complex whose remains are still so familiar to us. Exactly whether the actual bullion was used directly to pay contractors, or whether, as seems more likely, there was a rather more opaque relationship, is a matter for scholarly discussion, but there is no real dispute about the broad principle.

Banking practices including collateral/surety

We know of numerous references in the literature of individuals going to a banker, but what is meant by a 'banker' is probably closer to what most people understood by 'banker' forty years ago than now. It was cash based and strictly 'personal' banking. At one level the banker looked after the actual coins deposited for the depositor and (at least in principle) returned the same ones when requested. His contribution was to provide a safer and more convenient place than under the bed, and for this service he charged interest.

This, however, is not the full story, especially in respect of business needs, where cash deposited with the banker could be used to finance business expansion and trade. We know that at least the largest Greek banks could provide what we would today regard as a full range of traditional high street banking practice. Money was loaned out, at interest, as routine business. It was even possible, so as to avoid the need to carry large sums of cash abroad, for an individual to leave money on loan in Athens and carry a bank guarantee which would enable the bearer to obtain money (in the local currency) at the foreign destination.

Earned interest was an established concept, and standardised pretty well across antiquity. 1% per month, was often the starting point but bankers (and others) charged different rates according to circumstances, which might include making a distinction between lending to the principal of a deal or to a sub-contractor. It is well established that price changes through inflation existed – i.e. a market shortage pushed up the price of something (though a glut brought it down again), and that very generally over time (and especially in times of war) prices went up, but the current consensus among those who have addressed this issue in detail seems to be that the concept of inflation and its effects, as we assume we understand it, was not an issue of the magnitude that it is in our era.

However, a constant constraint upon the scale of these developments was the need for individuals to meet the banker personally to give proofs of identity and to make agreements. Bankers had to know the people they were dealing with and the system was dependent upon there being real cash deposited in the bank. Signatures and records depended upon the personal touch, too. At a time when mostly a skilled slave did all the writing under dictation, it all relied on personal contacts; there was no such thing as a signature to prove who one was; its nearest equivalent was a seal, but these were not as secure as a signature was later. So written records were very limited and, if a reusable slate rather than papyrus or soft wood were used, overwritable. This works in a relatively small city/society (by our standards) where virtually everyone who matters knows each other, and merchants and strangers depend on introductions to oil the wheels of business. But, when trade expands, personal contact becomes less and less feasible. Much of historical trade remained within the bounds of personally known contacts. In this context it is worth remembering that it was as late as 1891/2 that J C Fargo 'invented' the concept of the travellers' cheque; it was only then, as world trade globalised, that money transfer systems dependent upon personal introductions began to fail. We know from Demosthenes how records were kept:

For bankers are accustomed to write out memoranda of the sums they lend, the purposes for which sums are desired, and the payments which a borrower makes, in order that his receipts and his payments may be known to them for their accounts.

This sounds exactly like the kind of bank ledger that has been used in high street banking for centuries. Bankers' books provided a convenient vehicle for transacting and recording commercial affairs involving cash payments. Money would be deposited with the banker with an instruction for payment to be made to a specified payee. If the banker knew the payee, all that was necessary was the brief book entry. At a higher level, the promise to pay could be lodged before a court.

As now, bankers required security for loans. As merchants appear generally (see above) to have lacked capital, yet needed to purchase goods to trade, they were accustomed to take out loans, possibly from family and friends, and acquaintances – just as people do now, but equally from bankers. A number of Demosthenes' speeches discuss the 'ins and outs' of particular arrangements, and one speech actually uses a term best translated as 'jointly or severally', showing that this legal concept (which can cause difficulties in commerce now) was recognised and catered for 2,500 years ago.

Accounting and financing practices

By our standards the accounting practices in the ancient world were simple but they do seem to have been generally 'fit for purpose'. Ironically, the financial turmoil of 2008/9 throws up doubts as to whether the complexity of modern accounting and financial systems make ours 'fit for purpose'. Probably the truth is that any well thought out and transparent system, ancient or modern, is suitable for most transactions by reasonable people most of the time. Deliberate fraud is another matter and, as we all know, the ingenuity of fraudsters and those attempting to prevent their activities is becoming in our day increasingly sophisticated. In these terms, simpler systems may be more vulnerable than more complex ones – but anyone can always attempt and probably succeed with a scam if they try hard enough. It is not usually in the interest of an embarrassed party (especially if it is a corporate body) to publicise their naivety and losses, so the record of what actually happened in a scam is unlikely to survive.

This allowed, it is impossible to compare the complexities of modern financial engineering, which are so critical to the business cases underpinning many modern contracts, to the mechanisms available to the ancient Greeks. It is only in the last 100 years that financial "engineering" has become so complex and fast-paced. There remain issues of credit, money supply and interest which are still unresolved among some cultures today. There is plenty of evidence that in ancient Greece many of the pieces of the evolving financial jigsaw were in place – e.g., interest was paid on debt – but essentially commerce was a cash accounting business, which limited the scope for financial optioneering.

Particular issues affecting contracting in classical Greece were the relatively cumbersome numbering systems, and probable absence of a concept of double entry book accounting. The usual view is that double entry books were 'invented' in the mid-15th century, but some scholars think this might have been a re-invention of a lost classical practice. Double entry accounting is not vital when comparing the profitability of different enterprises or making rational economic decisions, but it does help and was common before computerised spreadsheets became the fashion.

Credits and debits may have been separately identified in classical Greece, but such accounting records as have been identified tend to show these in a mixed-up way. Today we find the use of columns a good device to enable us separately to identify debits and credit, but in antiquity many people appeared to have managed by finding the information they were searching for within the cramped confines of text steles, slates, tablets or rolls. Working on the back of an envelope is not unknown nowadays, even if other options are available, so we must be careful about the conclusions we might draw from a cramped text. However, for most people in most cultures, until very recently the cost of paper (or equivalent) was relatively great, so that our current acres of white space approach would not have been practicable; Leonardo's notes or Dickens' manuscripts are a reminder of how recent affordable white space is.

One benefit from the 'mixed-up' approach is that a less than precise – some might say muddled – structure can discourage people from thinking in the inflexible 'siloed' straight line way that so often blights modern financial systems. A limited or loose structure may mean it is easier to think flexibly – though it can equally mean no more than 'anything goes', or that what goes depends on how good an individual's memory recall is. (On reflection, given the limitations of so many of the 'expert knowledge' systems today, maybe individual memory is the only practicably reliable tool anyway!)

Perhaps most important, in trying to understand how the ancients would address the potential risks of a business trans-action, is the very different mindset of capitalist Western 21st century man – different, especially in the personal sphere, from that of his predecessors. In the UK at least (and until the 2008/9 crash led to some re-assessments), it has sometimes seemed that the prevailing climate among those with a little wealth (and those aspiring to wealth) has been to treat money as almost a virtual concept. Perhaps this is an inevitable consequence of using plastic cards and internet banking rather than piles of cash, albeit that in reality our 'cash' itself is also merely fiduciary money. Historically, this approach would be very odd. The practice of the richest elites in society is usually different from the 99% of less wealthy people, but in ancient times even the elite 1% would in principle, have obtained their wealth in cash, saved it in cash and transacted it in cash. If, for example, you bought/rented/ mortgaged a house or even if, as an elite citizen yourself, your duties required you to finance an army, you needed cash, which is bulky and heavy, and not such a notional concept as we are unintentionally inclined to think. Everyday living required cash, and this was the case for most people for most of history. In the UK today, legal rules against money-laundering and non-payment of tax have made it almost impossible for employees to be paid except by non-cash credit transfer to their banks, and then many increasingly use credit or debit cards for regular transactions, all of which tends to disconnect us from what day to day living carrying cash only would be like.

Thinking in terms of physical cash affects significantly how one addresses the practical issues of financing a project. There are good grounds for believing that the prospect of making money appealed to the Greek entrepreneur or philosopher as much as it does to the venture capitalist of today. For example, there is a story in Aristotle of the philosopher, Thales of Miletus, who used his astronomical skills to predict the weather, cornering the local olive market. Ancient entrepreneurs must have been able to calculate complex loan and profit rates or else they would not have been able to be successful. However, it is not only the scale that is different; it is the physicality of what is involved. This probably ensured that the planning of the Business Case (and so on) therefore remained more grounded in reality than may sometimes become the case now.

Conclusion

All the evidence, taken as a whole, seems to point to the view that those in the ancient Greek business community, despite all manner of differences in outlook and culture arising from the very different society in which they lived, assessed the risks and carried out their business activities in a way which is fundamentally similar to ours, and that we have not really improved upon the techniques they employed. One can identify simple purchases, more complex procurements, hires, leases, etc. And we have seen that insurance, bottomry especially, was understood and used to support trade, as were mortgages, as a way of raising money against a security.

9

PROCUREMENT STRATEGIES AND CONTRACT MANAGEMENT
Continued

Assembling the project team

Virtually all modern project management books stress the need for projects to be run by Project Boards. Their primary purpose is to keep focussed on the main objective and provide the overall conceptual and financial resources. They should appoint a Project Manager, who should be given specific but flexible powers to enable him or her to concentrate on delivering to time and cost, within the framework authorised by the Board. The genesis of many modern project disasters is the failure to observe the simple but difficult lesson that if reporting lines are confused or authorisations unclear, problems will occur. This idea is not new. Our evidence shows that the Greeks, too, set up Project Boards and Project Managers.

For an example from literature, in respect of the Parthenon building project (late mid-5th century BCE), Plutarch records that the celebrated sculptor Pheidias carried out the role we should now describe as senior Project Manager, for the whole enterprise. This may, of course, be no more than wishful thinking by Plutarch 600 years after the event (and the fact that excavations of the

Acropolis have revealed workshops dating to the construction phase which are now referred to as 'Pheidias' Workshop' is good marketing, but not necessarily good history). However, given Athens' constitution in the 5th century, we know there would have been a committee of elected citizens carrying out the role of Project Board responsible for the general strategic direction of the work, and no doubt including, for at least some of the time, Pericles, the leading politician and instigator of the whole project. So it is not unreasonable to surmise that there were one or more Project Managers reporting to them.

However, there is much better evidence for the detailed workings of the Project Board/Project Manager structure some 50-80 years later, in the early part of the 4th century. At Epidaurus, for example, a detailed study of the epigraphic evidence has shown that the 'Finance Board' carried out what we would now call project management during the construction phases. We have the names of those involved and we know that over a long period the individuals on the Board changed, but the structure continued. There is similar evidence from Delphi. There are also a number of the inscriptions of the same period which refer to management roles with supervisory responsibilities, including explicitly the 'architect'. There were, no doubt, many times when such control structures were not set up, but it is clear that the Greeks used what we too now regard as the 'correct' techniques. Given the possible Parthenon evidence of the previous century, and our reasonable knowledge of temple building going on elsewhere at about the same time, it is clear that large construction projects were typically set up with project teams to run them.

Most of the evidence is limited to building contracts. However, it is particularly interesting that of the few contracts for services that we have, at least one also uses supervisory project structures. Extending such controls to service contracts is something which was very much at the centre of procurement development in the

British public sector only a few years ago – indeed it was at the heart of initiatives such as setting up the Office of Government Commerce with its 'Gateway' review systems, and the Gershon Efficiency Review in 2004/5. However, as the Comptroller and Auditor General reported in December 2008, there are still omissions from this discipline in the public sector. Nor is it difficult to find otherwise thriving and excellent private sector companies where 'procurement' means professional purchasing for production materials only, and service contracts – e.g., Information, Communications and Technology (ICT), vehicles, facilities, professional services, etc., – are administered with no specialist input.

Developing contract strategy

In the absence of more precise evidence as to how this was addressed, I have identified one study only (Burford's) which attempts, albeit not using the words 'contract strategy' (or indeed 'procurement strategy'), and solely in the context of building works at Epidaurus, to outline how the strategy might have come about from an understanding of the management structure, the accounts, and the remaining architectural evidence. In addition to commenting upon the Epidauran evidence, it identifies epigraphical evidence from Tegea, Lebadeia, Athens and Delos which contributes to a view on how management teams may have planned work and then made amendments as the work progressed. One particular point which the evidence backs up relates to the general comments in literature to the effect that, in the aftermath of the Peloponnesian War, there was a shortage of skilled labour. It is possible that while Athens and Delphi might well have been able to have first call on such labour as did exist, less prestigious places, such as Epidaurus, would have had to take their place in the queue. This would explain both the length of time the project took and the piecemeal stage by stage methods used; the contracts were often very specific but limited – supply beams or stones, work up a particular relief, etc. Such a breakdown retains the primary controls with the client and is best suited to work which can be authorised only on a piecemeal basis.

However, two contracts (the Arsenal construction project in Athens and that for marsh drainage in Eretreia) provide evidence that more strategic contract specifications could be written, enabling (and here I speculate) the Project Manager/Architect to sub-let parts of the work if he so wished, rather than directly control it himself. The possibility that this approach might have been taken on suitable occasions is suggested by the existence (in the context of land leases) of a provision penalising unauthorised sub-leasing. The distinction between authorised and unauthorised sub-leasing (and for this purpose I am regarding the term 'sub-contracting' as conceptually synonymous) is that the client is able to expect that the sub-contractor is competent because he has taken a positive decision (authorisation) to use them on his work. Unauthorised sub-contracting means that all manner of people might be carrying out the work, giving rise to problems, especially on the quality of workmanship and (a concern nowadays) unknown people having access to a site.

A particularly interesting inscription which sets out detailed requirements relating to other contractors exists from Tegea, a small city in Arcadia, dating from about 350 BCE. This inscription can be interpreted in three ways. First, it could be an example of what we nowadays call a main contract, as it refers in detail to what may and may not happen if two or more contractors (sub contractors in our terms) are involved. This could be evidence of an overarching contract with some relationship with other contracts, which (given our present privity of contract concept) we would regard as sub-contracts. Second, we could interpret the 'main contract' slightly differently – perhaps as close to what we now call an enabling (or 'term', 'running' or 'umbrella') contract, meaning that it specifies the main terms of business governing the work, so that other work done and contractors mentioned, though in legal terms independent, need only to be authorised by simple orders. The third interpretation, which I think gives a better understanding of the Greek words in context, is that the inscription is just part of a general decree setting out the basis on which the state of Tegea wished to do business. Whether these terms were enforceable in practice we do not know. Whichever interpretation applies, it is good evidence that much thought was given to the practicalities of how contractual relationships could be managed.

It is common in much modern procurement to rely upon sub-contractors to carry out specialist parts of the work. Indeed, many modern routes to procurement are predicated upon the presumption that the procurement and contract strategies identify, and set up, the most appropriate mechanisms to ensure that all the parties to the project work to the same end. This is not as easy as it might sound. Because of the frequently encountered difficulties, there are today many specialist books setting out how this might be done, and in one of these I declare an interest, having been involved in the writing of Jon Broome's *Procurement Routes to Partnering – A Practical Guide*.[1] Sub-contracting is, of course, only part of contract strategy. Taken as a whole, the evidence we have means that it is possible to show that there could be occasions when the Greeks could flex their procurement methodologies according to need, just as we do.

---

[1] Broome, J, *Procurement Routes to Partnering – A Practical Guide* (Thomas Telford, 2002).

Risk assessment

Risk, whether financial, commercial, technical or physical, is an inevitable part of doing business. Commercial people today are accustomed to the idea of trying to identify in advance risk areas and to put in place mitigation strategies to minimise the possibility that potential risk issues will be encountered in practice. If risk cannot be eliminated or mitigated, then it must be "owned" so that in the event a risk event occurs in practice, it is clear who carries the responsibility to deal with it. In contractual terms risk can be allocated or divided between the parties. Those inexperienced in the real cut and thrust of procurement may well try to allocate all the risk away from themselves and regard this as shrewd. However many professionals today recognise that risks should generally be allocated to the party best placed to manage them in practice. Where a particular risk is recognised as significant but not controllable – e.g., the increased risk of flash floods from global warming – ideally the parties can work together, using whatever techniques they can to control or to mitigate the effects. In ancient Greece the possibility of earthquake activity or fire might have been seen as risks that were at least partly foreseeable. Risk mitigation mechanisms can be fairly simply broken down into different categories – the headings Financial, Contractual and Technical may be helpful. Each category does, of course, influence others, sometimes favourably and sometimes against one another. For example, a high risk of earthquakes means attempting to build stronger buildings, which in turn means more expense, which the contract tries to allow for by longer time schedules, etc.

Long experience, tradition and trial and error are all tools that have been used over the years by those responsible for construction works to assess the risks of building at certain strengths and at specific locations. It follows, therefore, that we should expect the Greeks to have made similar technical risk assessments. It is perhaps superfluous to state that the principal evidence that the ancients were able to undertake successful risk analysis continues to be the remarkable surviving ruins. Unfortunately in contract terms, no evidence of the actual calculations has survived (although theoretical reconstructions from the specifications that we do have might be feasible). I discussed financial risk in the previous chapter.

Plato also touches on risk in his *Republic*, though his concern seems to be a moralising one:

If a law commanded that voluntary contracts should be at the contractor's risk, the pursuit of wealth would be less shameless in the state and fewer of the evils of which we spoke just now would grow up there.

The inference is that risks were generally allocated in ways favourable to the client so that the contractor got a raw deal. This might be a personal reflection of Plato, who as a member of the landed elite may perhaps have acted as a financial guarantor and lost money on a deal that went wrong. The argument for favouring the contractor, of course, reflects the need to encourage entrepreneurs to accept risk so as to enable trade to take place in the first place. In fact my overall impression – I stress the word impression – of risk allocations within all the ancient Greek contractual texts I have read, is that the client (the state on many occasions) has cut a far better deal than one would expect it to in similar circumstances nowadays. (So either Plato's pleas were not heard or, because there is more competition nowadays, clients, rather than contractors, tend to get their way.)

Risks can be controlled by specific arrangements in the contract. An obvious area, still applicable, is for 'war risks', and putting in a war risks clause was common. Among the Greek city states warfare was endemic and usually life carried on regardless of the wars, with peace just the interlude between wars; this is doubtless why it was recognised as necessary to allow for war risks. The Tegean inscription discussed above suggests that the Tegeans fully appreciated the problems:

If war hinders [the completion of] any of the contracts, or damages any of the work already completed, the [Town Council] shall decide what to do.

As one might expect, the terms in particular contracts vary – one or two seem to me to be unduly onerous on the contractor, though conversely the Eretrian marsh drainage one is onerous for the client – but the majority appear to suggest that, in the event of war or destruction, the contractor's contribution to the client for damages for late performance will be reduced by half.

For other risk areas, including health and safety for example, we have to rely on the assumption that what we might nowadays call a 'commonsense' approach was taken. There is a story in Plutarch's *Pericles* about how concerned he was when one of the workmen fell from the Acropolis scaffolding and was injured. But, while it adds a human touch to what we know (and the point of the story is probably the miraculous recovery of the workman), it doesn't help us to understand anything about health and safety risk assessment. As it was only about 50 years ago that much specific attention became drawn to this area, the ancient Greek approach is in fact typical of how business has usually been done throughout the ages.

We do not know the extent to which specifications may have been adjusted to limit needless risks to the parties once, for example, more people had considered the issues, or after work had started, but on the evidence that the practice nowadays is to buy insurance (if practicable) to spread risks that cannot be engineered out of the project, it is interesting to note that forms of insurance did exist. The financial guarantor system (see above) was one way it was done, and it is surely reasonable to assume that it would be difficult to persuade people to sign up as guarantors if a risk was widely perceived as unacceptably great. There is also evidence in the orators of the insurance arrangements made in the maritime (bottomry) market, a well known and reasonably well understood class of risk.

Developing contract exit strategy

Except where properly experienced experts are involved at the start, it is unfortunately still commonplace today in many procurements that no proper thought is given to what should happen at the end of the process, and what should happen after that. At the simplest level, the procured items are acquired but no real thought has gone into the long-term financial implications of maintenance and replacement. In services contracting, the resources needed to enable decisions to be made, and action to be taken, to change contractors smoothly may not exist. All too often the exit strategy has to be invented on the hoof as the gap between an old contract ending and a new one starting yawns wide in front of the parties. As a result, unsatisfactory follow-on contracts – with equally unsatisfactory justifications for the decisions made – are frequently cobbled together at the last minute. For this reason it is salutary that, from our limited range of evidence, we have a number of contracts which deal with the contract terms on contract closure, subsequent actions and audit. One of them, from the town of Lebadeia, in fact reads almost like the text of the old UK government condition SC53, Pricing on Ascertained Costs (GC/Stores/1 (1979)) now DEFCON No 653. The entirely fanciful notion that SC53 was originally drafted by a Civil Service classical scholar who knew the Lebadeia texts is attractive!

With evidence of insurance for ships and cargoes going back 2,500 years comes also evidence of insurance scams. Sometimes they went spectacularly wrong. A Demosthenean speech contains the record of how two crooks had an insurance scam which would only work if the ship did not complete its journey. They tried to sink the ship by cutting a hole in it at night as it sailed along. Unfortunately, the sounds of sawing were heard and, in his rush to avoid being caught, one crook took a running jump into the sea, aiming at the rescue dinghy he had left trailing behind on a rope; but in the dark he missed his footing and drowned. Perhaps this can be categorised as an unsuccessful exit strategy. His accomplice boldly pretended nothing had happened, got to Athens and then claimed the cargo was his all along – and sued the real owners when they objected. We do not know the final outcome, but it seems that there were further complications, as some kind of out of court settlement may have followed, but of this we do not have evidence.

Developing a contract management plan

The interpretation of evidence that scholars have made, and my reading of the way the contracts seem to have been written, make it clear that detailed planning of the execution of contract activities was worked out in advance. The Tegean decree about contract arrangements mentioned above, for example, specifies actions to be taken if certain eventualities arise, and a number of other contracts also specify detailed change procedures.

Drafting specifications and requirements

As all modern procurement specialists know, if the specification is inadequate or wrong for the intended purpose, the chances of everything else being satisfactory are much reduced. Unfortunately, this is the area where precision, which takes time, is often sacrificed to a desire to have a contractor appointed quickly, and so give an illusion of progress. We can never know the extent to which this overarching human desire affected ancient contracting. What, however, we do know, via the reasonably detailed contracts which have survived, is that the Greeks were fully capable of writing adequate contract specifications. I have commented above on the quality and full adequacy of the Arsenal specification in Athens. I have also read a number of other specifications where either full or sufficient detail has survived for us to be certain that writing a proper specification (which a modern architect or project manager could work with) was fully within the capabilities of the ancient Greeks.

In respect of short specifications, the records of the Epidauran temple builders set out many of the tasks they needed performed as one line specifications. Many are for simple supply, where a short specification was adequate, provided there was no real doubt as to what was required. Others are less satisfactory – 'for working on the inscription' or, 'for fluting a column' are slightly minimal for what was involved, but presumably fit for purpose, especially if their main purpose was as accounting records. No doubt the parties discussed and agreed beforehand more precisely what was intended. Records from other locations confirm that the Epidauran practice was common.

The existence of these simple specifications may presuppose a higher level specification, to which perhaps the master craftsman (or, as we might call him, the Architect, worked), but we do not have this. A standard phrase which occurs in a number of the specifications is easily rendered into terminology familiar to modern practitioners as 'such as to satisfy the architect'. This rather vague terminology is in the UK now – at last – being challenged. How can one objectively define what is satisfactory, even to a "reasonable" architect? But to blame the Greeks for a phrase hallowed by time and argument over the millennia, while interesting, seems rather unfair. Although the word 'architect' is a transliteration of the word the Greeks used (ἀρχιτεκτος), it is misleading to read straight across from the Greek to our idea of an architect. 'Techne' (τεχνη) meant 'craft', and in terms of social status – whatever that might have meant in ancient Greece (and this is not the place to discuss this) – it is likely there would often have been a view that even a master craftsman (architect) was still essentially a paid craftsman rather than a gentleman (καλοςκἀγαθος – 'kaloskagathos') except of course, rather as was the case in British culture in years past, if an architect/craftsman/artist was internationally renowned for his skill, the usual social barriers became opaque – provided everything went well.

Other contracts we have include the list of tasks to be undertaken with a rather brief specification. Many of the examples, such as those for leases, are for activities which were no doubt routine in that line of business, hence there was no need for more detail.

An extant speech of the orator Lysias gives us a flavour of the kind of specification problems which can so frequently arise in that especially difficult to control category, the services/consultancy sector. In brief, the political grouping that temporarily took control of Athens in 410BCE (nowadays we might use the word 'junta') wanted the copies of the law kept in the market place refurbished and made up to date, and appointed Nicomachos and his team, on a daily rate, for what was expected to be four months, to 'collect copies of all the laws and inscribe them afresh on new stone'.

The work took six years and, after another five years, led to a court case. The political background is vital to our understanding of the case – essentially it was a period of civil war, and by the time the case went to court Nicomachos had been appointed by a group of people who had lost office (and in many cases their lives) and an entirely new political situation existed. The whole basis of the case was, therefore, very contentious and is currently subject to much scholarly debate. This fascinating material provides an opportunity to identify particular points relating to procurement, which are as follows:

First, strictly, Nicomachos was never a contractor, as according to Lysias he was 'appointed a commissioner'. In fact there is doubt as to whether his appointment could have been valid, but the procurement point which incidentally arises from this is whether or not an organisation (in this case the state) can enforce a contract against itself. A reasonably accurate analogy nowadays might be with organisations which place SLAs (Service Level Agreements) on other parts of their structures, apparently trying to mimic legally enforceable contracts. SLAs are notoriously difficult to control because they lack legal enforceability.

Second, since in ancient Greece the rule of law applied to contractual matters, it suited the parties, even during and after civil war, to use an apparent contractual arrangement as a vehicle for their dispute.

Third (and this is the specification point), Nicomachos justified the extra time he had taken by explaining how much larger a task it was than had been thought when he was commissioned. He had had to do extra research and, as he went along, the specification changed – new laws had been passed, others were deleted, etc. He even got involved in advising on the interpretation of the laws. He refused to hand over the completed work until his side of the story was told. Current practitioners can perhaps imagine slightly misleading headlines about, 'consultant rips off public sector' – and evidence of changing specifications, slack contract management, missed scheduled audits and the perils of daywork rates authorised by overworked but inexpert officials. All these are, unfortunately, extremely familiar problems today. The conclusion has to be that whereas simple specifications for supply contracts may have worked well, for more complex work problems could arise. Nothing changes.

Given the evidence of good specification writing that we do have, it is reasonable to suppose that all those regularly involved in particular trades, whether in building or elsewhere, knew from experience broadly what was required to achieve a particular end result, and the techniques and short cuts which were acceptable. The imposing evidence that still remains of ancient Greek building works presupposes the existence of sophisticated and well established ways of planning what was needed, and communicating those plans to the workforce. For the present argument, what is interesting is that the specifications which have survived look so familiar.

Establishing the Form of Contract (Contract Conditions)

This section is about the suitability of the detailed contract for its purpose, and can conveniently also include the part of the contract most often regarded as the 'legal' part – the terms and conditions of business. I have used evidence from both inscriptions (predominantly 'public sector') and literary records of court cases ('private sector') for this evidence, on the (unproven) assumption that since today we make no distinction in principle between business sectors, and use contract clauses in a fairly standardised way for all contracts, simply adjusting the precise words to particular cases, so too did the Greeks. The evidence I have identified, taken as a whole, has persuaded me that the Greeks seem to have used – whether they devised them or they evolved them from earlier examples we do not know – just about all the fundamental commercial legal concepts which we still regularly use in business.

A typical structure for a set of modern British international contract conditions will commence with definitions of who the parties are and what particular words are intended to mean, and then go on to refer to what has to be done – frequently set out in a detailed specification in another document – and by whom and when. It then covers major points such as early termination and damages, reporting systems, payment arrangements and liabilities. Grouped together, either at the beginning or the end, are a set of 'boilerplate' clauses (fundamental conditions common to virtually every properly drafted commercial contract). I have commented below in broadly this sequence.

Main Contract Clauses

1) Definitions of the parties involved and specification

The introductory sentences of well preserved epigraphic evidence that has come down to us routinely provides all this information, just as similar information is set out in the preamble of 21st century contracts. As now, the specification is often short, because work is frequently broken down so small that a brief description is all that is necessary. However, longer specifications do exist when needed (see above). Contractual problems often arise nowadays because the contract specification is not adequate for the purpose and because circumstances and ideas so often change after all has been agreed with the contractor. It would be surprising if the Greeks did not have similar problems. The story in Lysias is a case in point and there is a comment in Vitruvius (see below), in the context of how the Ephesians ran their contracts, which suggests that inadequate specifications have always been a problem. Conceptually therefore, the Greeks wrote and probably used and misused specifications just as we do.

2) Payment/Transfer of ownership

For many years it was thought that to be legally binding in ancient Greece the delivery of goods and payment had to be simultaneous, albeit that the practical implications of this (if fully thought through) must have meant that there would have been many transactions which did not meet this standard. This did not allow for the situations where, in Athens at least, credit sale appears to have taken place, and it is now also clear that borrowing from the banks to fund buying was not unusual. However, the precise implications in legal terms of what is understood to be happening when a party agrees to provide consideration in exchange for a benefit from another party is rightly a matter of full discussion for contract lawyers. The average purchaser, like the average high street shopper, gives very little thought to these details unless a significant purchase goes wrong, and the details of the relevant obligations have to be worked out from first principles. The day-to-day objective is simply to acquire the rights in the good being purchased and for this the agreed price will be paid. Just as happens nowadays for us, so in ancient Greece.

Transfer of possession is not the same as transfer of ownership, and we know of three legal cases about the problems this created, and examples of other real life complications – e.g., if a purchase is made with someone else's money, who is the ultimate owner?

Stage payment (payment for work completed in accordance with the contract up to a certain point) appears, as is the case today, to have been normal practice for many contracts. As the evidence of the typical contract displayed in the Appendix shows, the Greeks had established the usefulness of retention monies and tying part-payments to completed activities. This, of course, also allowed the stage payment system to be used against a contractor who had not met the contract requirements. We discuss this aspect further below. Conceptually, little has changed significantly since these classical Greek contracts were written. It would be interesting to know how effective these provisions actually were in practice. Maybe, as so frequently happens in modern experience, it was the case that, when it came to enforcing the provisions, it was found that variations (often unauthorised) from the written contract made by those performing the contract were such that the written provisions were either unenforceable or redundant.

An issue in complex modern contracts, with perhaps multiple or sectional deliveries to the purchaser's site, is assessing precisely when the ownership of part orders or part fabricated goods transfers to the purchaser. The seller does not want to lose ownership of his goods if the purchaser suddenly defaults, any more than the purchaser wants to risk having half of what he has purchased marooned at the seller's premises if the seller should call in his creditors. I have not tracked down any evidence which explicitly covers how to deal with such issues. (The situation recorded in the lead tablet from near Perpignan mentioned earlier is probably not this point specifically, as under that contract the purchaser would have received boats that worked, albeit not the number he wanted, if the contract had ceased at the halfway point.) Possibly in an economy where (to use modern terminology) sub-contracting for semi-manufactured goods would be rare, this was not an issue. It must also be remembered that, in principle, anything is negotiable if both parties agree, and the practicalities of transport meant that specifications were broken down into relatively small parts so that in general the scope for major pre-fabricated work was limited.

The most obvious exception to this is the statuary trade (i.e. the trade in statues). We know, from various sources discussed in the literature, that when a statue was required, at least one practice was for the contractor (usually the selected craftsman or artist) to select the stone he required from the quarry. He would presumably effectively sub-contract the early stone preparation but would manage the rough fashioning of the statue at the quarry, after which it would be transported to the site for finishing. We do not have any contracts setting out exactly what happened in particular cases, but commercial logic suggests that (unless exceptionally he could pass the risk back to the final purchasers) the contractor would take the risk of breakages or mishaps (including sinking when at sea) until handover of the completed article. There is a huge half finished broken statue in Naxos which perhaps shows (as do other examples in quarries) what could happen if a breakage occurred. It was just abandoned. We know that when Michelangelo and other renaissance sculptors were seeking the right marble, there had to be negotiations over who would pay for disasters; the obvious person to take the risk was the contractor, who would no doubt have tried to cover himself by charging what we would now call a risk premium, so there may well have been a similar practice in ancient Greece.

Retention of title by the seller (even after payment) has at various times in the recent past been an issue in modern procurement, but we have no evidence which appears to relate to this, and in an essentially cash economy, such as that operated by the ancient Greeks, issues of this kind may not have arisen. But even in a cash economy provable arrangements have to be made so that, for example, the timing of the cash transfer and the transfer of ownership of the good being purchased can be settled; so too are issues such as the proof that the seller is the owner of the good (and therefore has the right to sell it) and mechanisms such as advances, deposits, staged and deferred payments. These are all well evidenced in the literature and, indeed, are no less real in cash based economies than in our modern economy where cash money has almost become a virtual concept.

Proof that the money has been paid is usually given by the transfer of the good, often today with a piece of paper signed by the seller confirming the receipt of the consideration and thus discharging the liability between the parties. This deals with simple cases, but when anything more complicated or long-term is involved – as applies, e.g., to land or property leasing – some form of security or guarantee is required. As already discussed, in the context of risk management, guarantor arrangements to meet these needs were commonly used.

Two contracts, one from Delos and the other from Lebadeia, are especially interesting in respect of confirmation of payment in that they provided explicitly for final cost reconciliations and immediate audit. Unfortunately, we do not know whether this was normal practice for significant contracts – one might speculate that it was. Aristotle mentions the perils of advance payments in a possible crack at the Sophists (literally 'wise men' – in reality itinerant lecturers who taught for a fee) when he wrote that:

> if a man, being paid in advance, fulfils none of his engagements ..... he is rightly held chargeable; for he does not perform his contract. But the sophists perhaps are compelled to adopt this plan [of payment in advance] for otherwise no one would give anything for what they know.

It is interesting that even today education, training and conferences are virtually the only services for which it is still conventional to pay the full fee in advance of fully satisfactory delivery. Certainly, it is conventional to buy, for example, travel or entertainment in advance of delivery, but these have very specific deliverables, which is different from the education sector. If one does not travel, the chances are, depending upon the terms, that one can obtain a refund, or a later booking. It is virtually impossible – there have recently been attempts in court but I believe they have failed – to obtain a refund if, e.g., one does not pass one's exams or, at the end, one decides a conference was not worth the fee. Payment in advance is the 'custom of the trade' and presumably this continues because, as was the case in Aristotle's day, the absence of a substantive physical deliverable makes it very difficult to price, in a way acceptable to those who end up dissatisfied, a specific monetary value against an educational outcome.

The converse to advance payments is sales on credit – where the purchaser cannot provide the consideration (usually money) at the time but, for all manner of reasons, the objective of the purchase has to be met. The Greeks did this too.

Leaving aside the niceties of the legal position – important though they are – the key outcome of this brief discussion is that there is sufficient evidence to be able to conclude that the problems of scheduling payments to deal with the availability (or otherwise) of money, and the consequent problems of ownership transfer that arise, were recognised by the ancient Greeks, and that conceptually similar contract clauses were written to cover each circumstance.

3) Warranties

There is evidence from Athens, Knossos in Crete and Abdera in central Greece, that warranties (similar to guarantees) of fitness for purpose existed. If a latent illness came to light within a specified period in recently purchased cattle or mules, one could get one's money back. It is interesting, too, that this forward-looking provision also applied to a category of good which is not now on sale (as such) in regular commerce – the purchase of a slave – and perhaps ironic, given our 21st century sensibilities, that if what Plato wrote in his treatise *Laws* was at any time real law, as opposed to a theoretical approach, a subtle distinction in respect of slaves was also made between business to business (B2B) contracts and business to consumer contracts (B2C). Plato argued that if, as a private citizen, you bought a slave and you discovered a defect in him/her that had not been declared at the time you bought, the law should permit you to return the slave and demand your money back. He went on to say that this rule should not apply for sales between merchants (we would now say B2B) as merchants should be expected to understand the commercial risks.

In the building and allied trades the judgement as to whether, say, a wall has been properly built, is a matter for acceptance or non-acceptance by the Project Manager or Architect in charge. Once acceptance has been given, that is the end of the matter except, of course that, in time, defective work not apparent at the time of acceptance, may become evident. Trying to provide for, and when applicable, resolving latent defect issues is a large part of modern works contracting, though the parties tend to discuss the issues under the heading 'damages' rather than 'warranty'. See below.

4) Breach and damages

What can an aggrieved party do to put matters right if contractual obligations are not being carried out as specified? I suggest that as a consequence of the process I drew attention to in my introduction, ancient notions of honour and personal liability (albeit one may suspect possibly honoured more in the breach and by tradition than in practice) transmuted, by virtue of the existence of a formalised contract, into the semi-separate and independent idea of a formalised obligation, actionable, if necessary, by the courts. It was, therefore, possibly but a short step to devise the concept of contractual damages. However it came about, and regardless of the precise legal definition (not the topic of this study) the concept of a right for damages is well attested in the evidence.

In modern English contractual practice there are well established concepts for breach and damages. Briefly, breaches not going to the heart of the contract are regarded as simply breaches of terms or warranties. Restitution is usually a matter for negotiation, but, in principle, the courts would not (of course it depends on the precise issue) see such a failing as acceptable grounds for repudiation of the contract as a whole. However, for a fundamental breach of conditions of contract, full termination is the remedy. Often contracts have Termination or Break conditions (frequently for the benefit of the purchaser only) which set out systematic mechanisms for the resolution of alleged breaches. In these cases, damages at large may be payable to the aggrieved party, but, in cases of dispute, it must be shown that the party seeking damages have taken reasonable steps to alleviate the costs of non-performance, and claims for remote and consequential damages are regularly struck down if they are disputed in the courts. There is also the practice for providing for delay damages in a contract, which is held to be a simpler mechanism for resolving breaches – especially delays in completion – equitably.

However, in English Law another principle applies: damages may not be punitive. Their purpose is to restore the parties to the presumed equitable position at which they commenced the contract. Hence the inadmissibility of remote and consequential damages. Countries subject to different versions of US or Roman Law (e.g., many EU states) do, I understand, in some circumstances give more scope to charge penalties to those who have not met contract requirements than does English Law, but my impression is that the scale of compensation ancient Greek contractors seem to have been prepared to accept, according to the inscriptions, would be unusually onerous. This perhaps points to harsher cultural expectations for failure than modern competitive markets are prepared to allow; conversely, it might even imply that failure (a fairly common circumstance nowadays) was very rare – but we cannot know.

As regards the detailed English Law comparison, the Greek evidence is clear as regards the concept of restitution, but not conclusive as regards the 'at large' and 'reasonable' issue.

Detailed clauses in the epigraphical evidence of 'public sector' bodies contracting with the 'private sector' show that, in the event of the contractor not performing the contract requirements 'to the satisfaction of the architect', up to double compensation, especially in cases of negligence, was enforceable. These are probably best interpreted as punitive penalties, but we cannot be sure. There is also evidence showing that where the architect decided work was unsatisfactory, it was taken away from one contractor and placed for completion with another. I have not identified evidence which enables me to comment on the extent to which damages could be claimed after the work had been accepted as apparently meeting the requirements – i.e., latent damages coming to light a long time after the contract has been completed.

In modern contracting, if it is not just the terms of the contract but a wider legal obligation which has been breached (e.g., a competition, environmental or health and safety offence) the offending party may be liable to make financial compensation to the state. The law has recently been changed so that, in the most negligent or deliberate cases, corporate responsibility cannot protect individuals from personal penalties. This is a very recent modern development, but the underlying concept, that in certain circumstances the state ensures that individuals responsible for contractual breaches have personal responsibility for their actions, is actually a reversion to an ancient Greek notion about responsibility which has not previously applied in English law.

An extreme example relates to the Greek attitude to suicide. Aristotle, writing about suicide and unjust acts, identifies the state, not the family, as the injured party whom a suicide has wronged. It may be, of course, that this view is just a philosophical point and not typical of the times, though the notion that a man owes a contractual debt, as it were, to live so as to contribute to the success of his state, links well with the Greek idea of personal contractual obligation which Bresson identified. Until the recent change in the law, the legal position in England meant that those in business responsible for contracting did not have to worry much about the state becoming involved if their personal actions resulted in an individual's death or injury within a contract. It will be interesting to see how the change affects attitudes over time.

5) Incentivisation

A formal incentive in a contract (as opposed to the informal extra benefits to both parties that may result from building good relationships or by exceeding the specification requirements) can be seen as the *quid pro quo* of damages. Until recently, English contractual practice, particularly in the public sector, seems to have been driven primarily by the premise that the contractor (often less powerful than the client) should be punished for a breach. Provided he delivered according to the agreed requirement, he received the contract sum. If he were late, for example, damages would ensue. However, as power structures have changed and private sector win-win concepts have become more widely known and accepted, the idea that both parties can gain if the contract goes better than the mean performance has become more widespread. This is the target or incentivisation contract, whereby for a given improvement such as quality, quantity or timescales, both parties share the benefits in negotiated proportions. This way of working is considered best modern procurement practice.

There is at least one well known ancient example. According to Vitruvius, Ephesus was known for having a special law which against all the odds evidently worked – if it had not it would not have been identified as exceptional. It was a simple incentivisation contract and worked as follows: when the architect had drawn up his plans and estimates of costs, he handed a copy to the city fathers for safe keeping. Critically, and unusually however, he was also obliged to assign all his own property to them too, for the duration of the contract. If the work was done to time and cost, the architect/project manager/contractor was rewarded with public honours and publicity. If the final cost was up to 25% more than the estimate, the city paid up to that amount. However, above that amount, the architect's property was forfeit to the extent necessary to meet the extra costs.

This can probably best be seen as a form of liquidated damages, as the amount for which the defaulting architect was liable was, in principle, a pre-arranged known figure, and unless the architect owned huge property, in terms of city finances as a whole the amount of money forfeit would probably be considerably less than the city's loss. However, in terms of the individual, the arrangement would have had the effect of wiping him out. In personal terms, therefore, the risk the architect took on would, in present day English terms, be seen as a penalty, and thus probably inequitable. This, however, is a view expressed from the expectation of limited liability. There are even today a fair number of sole traders who take on unlimited liabilities in the expectation that they will prevail. Until recently, Lloyd's names were a well known elite in this category. Reverting to the ancient example, the question does arise as to when the Ephesus arrangement might become a disincentive. But moonlight flits have always been the escape route for those who anticipate trouble.

Vitruvius seems to be certain that this law only existed (and, presumably, worked) in Ephesus, for he continues with a lament which rings true down the years:

If only we had such a law, not only for public but for private buildings too. Then unlicensed cowboys wouldn't get away with shoddy work, contractors would be more careful in controlling and declaring the real costs; owners wouldn't find themselves in unexpected debt, etc., etc.

It was a feature of Greek cities that benefactors to the city were recognised by grants of ἀτελεια [*ateleia*] freedom from taxation. It appears to have been common practice to recognise such grants publicly by setting up an inscription, and as these inscriptions have survived we know something of them. Ateleia issues generally are outside the scope of this book, but four of the contracts I identified record that contractors will receive freedom from taxation for the import and export of their tools within defined time limits; so this practice would seem to have been a fairly commonly used contract incentive for timely completion of the work. The advantageous tax allowances and reliefs which modern states sometimes offer are perhaps the nearest modern equivalents to this practice. Often too with ateleia went ἀσυλια [*asulia*] giving the contractor the safety status of a suppliant within the city state. Such a notion does not come easily to us, but perhaps 'freedom from being charged with unreasonable liabilities' is a way of reflecting this idea.

6) Confidentiality

As I have shown above, for the Greeks a public record of a contract or lease on an inscription appears to have been a routine practice, at least when what we should now categorise as 'public' bodies are involved. The evidence provides contract detail which we would now often regard as confidential – restricted to the contracting parties only. From this it certainly appears that the Greeks took an entirely different view from us on what is and is not a matter for the public record, and nowhere during my researches have I come across an indication that the Greeks had any concept of contractual confidentiality. By comparison with what seems to be the remarkably similar approach the ancient Greeks had to contracting, I suggest this difference also has implications as regards the way the parties looked at accountability and audit. I discuss this, and the wider concepts of transparency in contract generally, in much more detail in the final chapter, as it may be that in the area of confidentiality, thinking about ancient Greek practice could help us to reflect on our accustomed ways of doing business and reconsider how suitable for purpose our present practices are.

7) Law, Territoriality and Arbitration

In modern contracting, provisions covering these areas are routine. The nature and requirements of trade between states is no doubt the reason that, certainly by the 5th century, the Athenians, and we may assume other Greeks involved in trading, were familiar with the same problems and came up with similar solutions. One of the first things new purchasing people learn on any Contract Law course is that, when writing a contract, it is essential that the parties agree whose legal system is to apply should the contract lead to legal action. Usually those in Britain automatically choose English Law (though, of course, north of the border Scottish Law is quite often applied). And for obvious reasons, all try to avoid making contracts subject to an unfamiliar legal system.

As Greek city states traded with other Greek city states, they no doubt came across the practical problems of trying to reconcile different legal systems. They also appreciated that if the terms of the agreement were written down it stopped arguments about who had agreed what, and this included specifying whose law applied. The details of contracts that have survived, mainly in disputed cases covered by the orators, cover topics that are all familiar ones nowadays: who, what, where, when, how much; what the penalty is if a party defaults, whose law, whose arbitration, and what insurance arrangements.

There was a law on Arbitration which applied to private contracts. Demosthenes (again) said:

If people disagree with each other about private contracts and they wish to choose someone as arbitrator, it is permitted for them to choose whoever they want to serve as arbitrators. When they choose someone together, they must stick with the judgement made by this person, and they can no longer transfer the charges from this person to another court, but let the judgement made by the arbitrator be valid.

There are many other references to Arbitration procedures in private disputes, but we do not know if Arbitration could be used in a dispute where one of the parties was a public body. My impression of these contracts is that the contracts were written by the state and the state called the shots. Perhaps in practice it did, but if contractors felt badly treated would they be willing to take on a contract with the state next time? We have no means of knowing.

The principle of Arbitration on this basis has not really changed, albeit that in the contractual area (though not necessarily in human resources disputes) Arbitration is now in many ways so similar to a full court case that arbitration has been reinvented as Adjudication. The last sentence in the quotation above shows that the problem of the party who is unwilling to accept that the Arbitrator's decision is final was as familiar then as now.

8) Limitation

It is well established in English Law that once the parties have agreed that a contract has been fully discharged (I am using the word 'agreed' in a simple sense in this context; often disputes are about what people meant by 'agreed'), there is only so much time during which the contract issues can be re-opened. For major contracts certain liability clauses affecting physical things may survive for many years (e.g., defects liabilities for, say, construction; and in the nuclear industry certain liabilities survive for many, many years, backed by the state) but, in general, the Limitation Acts lay down six years from the last contractual activity for a simple contract, or twelve years for a contract under seal.

The Athenians had a law which appears to have put a time limit of five years in respect of whether an action was admissible at law and there are a number of examples of this being a key factor in a dispute. This is not the same, of course, as certain evidence that the concept of limitation applied to contracts as such, albeit that it suggests that the concept of a time limit on actions at law did exist, and so is an attractive speculation in respect of contracts.

9) Entirety

Today, when negotiation of a contract has been protracted, with various relevant (and less than relevant) documents, it is good practice to ensure, by an entirety clause, that the parties agree that the contract document is specific to the agreement and covers what is intended and only what is intended.

Whether or not such considerations were explicitly considered by the Greeks is not clear from the evidence that we have, but in one contract where the actual wording of the Agreement between the parties is preserved, the last sentence comes fairly close to this concept:

> And in regard to these matters [above] nothing shall have greater effect than the agreement.

Elsewhere in this Demosthenean speech itself, the following interesting statement is made:

> The Agreement does not permit anything to have greater effect than the terms contained in it, nor that anyone should bring forward any law or anything else whatsoever to contravene its provisions....

Possibly this should be read as a hopeful gloss on the precise wording in the contract, on exactly the same basis as such a sentence is sometimes nowadays written in a contract, since it may be worth writing it in even if, in terms of strict law, there are grounds to suspect that a court would not uphold the precise wording. The importance of taking into account the whole contract and its intention is perhaps incidentally stressed in a sentence from another contract (Demosthenes again) which is really focused on other points:

> You ignore this clause of the agreement, but having first violated its provisions by failing to put goods on board you raise a dispute about a single clause in it, though you have by your own act rendered [the latter clause] null and void.

10) Agency

How a society caters for Agency in contract is an interesting issue. Plato had a particular angle on the point when he wrote (in the context of an ideal state):

> We shall need agents to handle the export and import of goods, whom we call merchants. How are its citizens to exchange the products of their labour? .... they will buy and sell ..... and that will require a market, and a currency as a medium of exchange ..... a (less fit) class unsuitable for other work – who sit in the market place and buy and sell.

However, for most citizens, merchants would be regarded as the principals in a contract and the idea that, for the layman, the person one sees buying and selling has the power and right to carry out these actions was clearly well established in antiquity. Everyday shopping could hardly be carried out without this concept, except, of course, that it is not unreasonable to speculate that many routine purchases might have been carried out by servants or slaves of the household on the basis, perhaps, that a reckoning-up and payment would be carried out by the master every few days. (For large establishments, surely the steward would do this task – which brings back again the idea of Agency.) Turning to business models, in modern parlance we could look upon such purchases as being made by agents of the 'corporate' household, perhaps the equivalent of modern employees.

Returning to Plato: his view assumes, of course, that the merchant has paid his supplier for the goods he is selling and is selling them as principal, and most of us just carry on on this basis, until we come across some horror situation – e.g., the car we have just bought was stolen so our seller doesn't have the right to sell to us. Similar kinds of issues – especially regarding who had the right to do what – may well have clogged up the relevant courts in Athens.

The case which perhaps most nicely outlines the legal position of Agency is Hyperides' speech 'Against Athenogenes' and the speaker's unfortunate experiences when trying to buy a perfume shop. The actions of one of the shop managers, Midas, had resulted in the shop having big debts. Midas's personal status as a slave adds complexity to the case, but the relevant point is that it was established Greek Law that a principal, in this case the speaker (if he were proven as the new owner), was liable for the debts of his agents. And Midas's debts would have ruined him.

Other aspects of commercial management
Establishing the pre-qualification, qualification and tendering procedures
Appraising suppliers (and Competitive Bidding)
Drafting tender documents
Evaluating tenders
I have not traced anything which can be taken as evidence about these four areas of modern 'best practice' procurement, which take considerable time, effort and energy in modern commercial "deals". I therefore review these areas together as they are linked issues. It is reasonable to expect that the Greeks, like ourselves if we plan to have work done on contract, would have established which contractor was most likely to meet their requirements. We know from the inscriptions we have that they could specify what they wanted. However, given the numerically much smaller number of people in a particular city likely to be capable of doing a particular job, the numbers of family and other relationships which might condition the choice of contractor, and the effect of different cultural values, the scope for competition between contractors is likely to have been relatively restricted for many of the smaller communities. As I speculated above, it may also have been lack of competition which led to the client rather than the contractor being able to lay off contractual risk. Of course,

the chances of the work being of such a nature that any specific evidence might be identified now is negligible. To attract more competition it was necessary to seek assistance from contract workers from other places.

Leading cities did this, attracting for prestigious work panhellenically renowned sculptors and artists. Athens is the obvious example, but many others, including those already mentioned in various paragraphs in this book, brought in outsiders for the kinds of activities whose records might perhaps be known to us nowadays from inscriptions or literature. No doubt it sometimes suited those who had arrived to do high profile work (especially if they were not themselves the leading lights, but just sound craftsmen who moved as opportunity beckoned) to stay and perhaps compete for simpler tasks against the local labour. One can speculate on all manner of variables. In the maritime market, transportation between cities being the essence of trade, active competition between shipowners is perhaps a reasonable assumption, especially on the main routes.

Sadly, there is not much specific evidence to bring to bear for any of the topics under this subheading. We have literary and inscription evidence that public bidding for contracts was done in the marketplace (though we do not know how it was done), and there is no reason to suppose this was other than a common practice for at least major state contracts. It is equally reasonable to assume that, except when special circumstances arose (e.g., we know an unusually high bid for a tax farming contract was a deliberate ploy to break up a cartel, so it was not just a commercial decision), competition would lead to offers such that decisions could normally be made on the basis of cheapest price or best value. We can also speculate that for highly prestigious work, especially where artistic and creative skills were involved, simple monetary costs might be less important than ensuring that the result met overall value for money criteria; as is the case today.

It can be argued that the best architect or artist available brings unique skills to a project. No records survive of how the full range of activities under the headings above were actually carried out.

Negotiation

Negotiation techniques vary from culture to culture, and the roots of the Greek words for buying and selling relate to bartering and negotiations. The historians, poets and epigraphic evidence tell us quite a lot about negotiations between states, and their outcomes. However, as a commercial negotiation is essentially a transient event, we have nothing directly relating to commerce. As in all negotiation, the end result would have been the best deal both parties were prepared to accept.

Awarding the contract

The existence of the contracts and the fragmentary stories about them that have survived are the pragmatic proof that contracts were awarded. We also know what constituted legal proof of contract award.

Downstream or post-award activities

Changes within the contract
Service delivery management
Relationship management
Contract administration
Assessment of risk
Purchasing organisation's performance and effectiveness review
Contract closure

A number of the situations about which the orators speak are concerned with issues which took place after the contracts were awarded and might therefore be categorised under these headings. However, I have felt that the points they were about fitted more suitably under headings elsewhere in the book. The epigraphical evidence, however, is more specific. Unfortunately, we do not have recorded on stone (after the main text) short notes saying, in effect, 'later we agreed to do such and such extra work', or, 'revised price for y', etc., but what we do have are procedures laid down to cover foreseen eventualities. Thus many of these contracts and leases have entries such as: 'if the contractor does a specified act (or omission) then x will happen; but if not, z will happen'.

This is similar to current best practice where procedural options are written into the contract, but is unlike many current less well drafted contracts which typically just specify what is needed. Then, as now, there must have been many occasions where an event occurred which could not equitably be covered by what was in the contract. Presumably, as is the case nowadays, and as part of Contract Management, the parties conferred and worked out the best way forward in the light of their overall relationship, which might, on occasion, lead to the courts. But this is just speculation. It is a pity we shall never know what really happened, granted that only disasters make good stories. There are, however, a number of other important aspects of procurement upon which comment is needed, and these are covered in the next Chapter.

10

AUDIT REQUIREMENTS; FRAUD; QUALITY

Audit and fraud

In the UK it is today accepted good practice for there to be close audit scrutiny of contracts. In many organisations procurement departments are audited almost continuously, both by internal and external auditors, and there are strict rules on what staff may or may not do. How useful or effective such checks may be is not the subject of this discussion.

If it were not for the evident need the Greeks felt to record what the state and individuals had agreed publicly we would not have the epigraphical records of contracts that have survived, nor the evidence of the checks that were scheduled to be done. They provide the hard evidence of public accountability which otherwise would only exist in the literary record, albeit that it is the literary record (Aristotle especially) which set out the audit purpose of the inscriptions. Unfortunately, most ancient accounting records were meant to demonstrate, and their publication to advertise, the selfless responsibility with which the administration had discharged its office, rather than provide evidence of the contracts which so often provided the means through which the administration carried out its civic responsibilities.

The famous story of Archimedes and the bath tub recorded by Vitruvius is in fact about auditing and fraud. The displacement of mass outcome was the by-product of Archimedes being asked to audit and investigate a suspected case of contract fraud: was the king of Syracuse's gold crown made of pure gold or was it an adulterated metal mix from a crooked goldsmith – as indeed Archimedes' displacement test proved? It would be nice to know what the contractual outcome of Archimedes' discovery of fraud might have been – no doubt the contract was repudiated, and possibly Sicilian fraud remedies left the goldsmith wishing he hadn't tried it on!

The fundamental rationale for any contract is the need to specify explicitly the arrangements between the parties, so that each is clear as to their obligations and has a defence against differences of opinion as to what was agreed. Such a way of thinking can only arise if at least one party is alive to the possibility of, if not fraud exactly, sharp practice – and that is perhaps only the downward slope towards fraud. It regularly astounds me, as a procurement specialist, to discover, as I do in the course of my day job, examples even now of trusting or gullible people who have made commercial arrangements without any apparent understanding of the range of risks involved. Often they are lucky; sometimes not.

It certainly appears that the Greeks took what we might regard as a realist's view of good faith and trust. This was famously set out later by the Roman poet Virgil, commenting upon the 'gift' of the treacherous wooden horse of Troy ('I fear the Greeks, especially when they bring gifts'). Bribery, too, was a serious offence in ancient times, just as it is now. It is important not to read too much into this (the distinction between realistic scepticism and mistrust is subtle) but worth recalling the words put by Thucydides into the mouth of Pericles when he is arguing the importance of democratically free Athenians choosing what is right over expedience:

> Even if he is patriotic but not able to resist a bribe, then this one fault will expose everything to the risk of being bought and sold.

Inevitably, many of Demosthenes' 'private sector' speeches are about what one party considered to be fraudulent behaviour. We do not usually know what the outcomes were or, more particularly, what the participants thought of the outcome, which is the real test. Suffice it to say that the courts daily address the same problems now in respect of contractual agreements. However, our modern assumption that commercial confidentiality should normally take precedence over transparency of process and information, and the complexity of modern business, does seem to lead to fraud trials which are subject to byzantine procedural hurdles, and the outcomes are often seen as unsatisfactory.

Quality

In recent years, ensuring that specified quality is actually delivered in practice has become a very sophisticated matter, through a combination of regular progress reporting and by precise measurement. This monitoring and measurement is usually underpinned by modern management reporting systems. However, it is less than forty years ago that many organisations relied primarily on armies of Inspectors to ensure that what had arrived in the warehouse, or what was constructed on-site, was what had been ordered. In principle, this situation was not much changed from the process which must have existed throughout history and before the existence of mass manufactured goods. Specific individual inspection, albeit assisted by modern tools, is still the only foolproof way of assessing the acceptability of work done in some areas, e.g., building or services contracts.

Excepting the story of Archimedes' and the King of Sicily's

crown (which as well as being a record of fraud is a story of how a quality check can be done), I have not been able to identify specific examples of quality issues. There are many references, as there are throughout history, to goods received (e.g., warlike *materiel* or food) not being up to the expected standard. Homeric heroes depended for their survival upon the special qualities of their divinely-artificed weapons, and if the weapons failed assumed that the gods were against them. Whether real ancient Greeks elevated failure in this way or, more likely, just blamed poor manufacture, we cannot be sure, though blame culture and the courtroom are more likely. Suffice it to note that quality and specification problems continue to be in the news regularly in the context of present day conflicts (e.g., Afghanistan) and on the domestic front (e.g., the well publicised recalls that car manufacturers make every so often).

It could well be that quality was so much of an 'accepted risk' in ancient Greece that no special mention was needed. But there is plenty of relevant material in the sense that there are examples of contracts which spell out the consequences to the contractor if he does not achieve the contract objective. These were discussed in the section on damages in Chapter 9. It is only speculation, but an attractive idea, to suppose that Demosthenes' father's factory delivered goods to an acceptable standard, since otherwise it would surely have been very difficult for Demosthenes to have maintained in court in his maiden speech (after he had attained his majority and wished to recover his rights as owner from the executors of his father's will, who had spent his inheritance) that the factory was a reasonably successful business providing good quality products. But this is not precise evidence, and we do know that much of the skill of an orator then (and perhaps now) is to paint the picture he wishes his audience to imagine.

11

CONCLUSIONS

I now attempt to answer the questions I raised in Chapter 2.

a) Did the Greeks think of procurement as a process, or just a transactional activity?

The question is important, but in some respects the answer is self-evident. Only by treating procurement as a process can sensible complex contracting (as opposed to simple order placing, which is transactional) be done. The various examples of Greek contractual practice commented upon in this book point to the answer to this question being that the Greeks understood procurement as a process.

The physical evidence of successful complex project work still exists, in that we have parts of the contracts for structures that we know from archaeological evidence – e.g., at Athens the rebuilding of the Long Walls in the 390s; the Prostoon; the Arsenal; the buildings at Epidaurus, Delphi and Delos, etc. However, Alison Burford's study forty years on is still in my view the only one (other than, I like to think, this book, which is not a scholarly study in the same sense) that has, even if incidentally, considered the management structure of ancient Greek procurements from the perspective of the real practicalities of what would have been necessary to make a project happen on the ground – or, to put it another way, to consider the procurement process.

In this book I have tried to fill in the inevitable gaps in the evidence by calling upon my expectation of how procurement specialists today might tackle issues. The problem is that contract words are a single part only of the process. What happened afterwards, before the parties were fully discharged of the burden of their contract obligations? Experience of procurement indicates that during the execution of even the best run projects, problems would have arisen which the procedural options in the contract would not have addressed. We know from accounting records that if work did not meet the architect's criteria it could be taken from one contractor and handed to another. However, in the absence of precise evidence, all we can do is assume that, as a well-structured framework for contracting did exist, it is likely that the solutions to problems would have been tackled in very much the same way as good project managers would tackle similar problems nowadays – rational analysis and an attempt to find the next best option.

In the event that the parties were unable to agree a way forward, we know from the literature that the concept of arbitration existed in what I have shorthanded as 'private sector' contracting. We also know that disputes of all kinds went to court. People do not do this if the problems are just about simple and transactional business.

b) Did different types of purchasing attract different approaches?

Chapter 2 drew attention to the distinction between purchasing and procurement. Having decided upon buying the goods and services required, did the Greeks approach the formation of individual contracts in different ways? The specific objective evidence is limited, as discussions on contract formation do not survive. However, this not to say that there is not evidence of a more circumstantial kind which is sufficient to enable us to make an assessment on the basis of probabilities. Thus, while we have contract specification evidence for large and small building works (e.g., Athenian Arsenal project versus small tasks at Epidaurus), it is reasonable to suppose that setting up the contract to build the Arsenal took more time and effort than a contract to pay someone to supply just the necessary wood or stone. In the same way, the few services contracts we have provide distinctive specifications.

One contract included tax exemptions during the period of the contract as part of the deal. If the contractor refused work assigned to him, he and his team lost these exemptions.

But the words used, 'if he refuses work', are themselves interesting contractually as they suggest the contract was written not just as a specified list of tasks (as one might expect) but that work would be allocated on an 'as and when' basis. This means that the contract cannot be a straightforward contract like others, but is what in the UK today is known as an enabling (or 'term', 'running' or 'umbrella') contract – one where agreed conditions and rates apply, but which in simple terms is effectively a separate small order every time a task is identified. A contract from Tegea may also be of this kind. To conceive of and to write contracts in this way, so as to be able to meet differing situations, is evidence of a sophisticated and professional approach to contracting.

The consultancy contract for the scribe Spensithios is different again, as it has provisions to cover his family. This is almost an employment contract with personal benefits. Conceptually, a modern day equivalent might be a chief executive's 'contract package'. Different again are the contracts for leases which deal with the special circumstances which apply to operating a contracted-out religious shrine for example.

Just as today, the individuals involved in property transactions, building works, services, the import/export trades and everyday buying and shopping, would have brought different motivations, skills and approaches to each contract. In principle, there is no reason to suppose that those involved then would not have approached each contract opportunity as we do. They went shopping and simple transactional issues applied (unless it was for a major item such as cattle or a slave, where there might be a warranty). If they wanted to lease or purchase a house, the format was well established, and it seems that fairly straightforward contracts were the norm. If works for public buildings were required, yet different skills were needed. Those who had the greatest entrepreneurial tendencies might become involved in, for example, the import/export markets. As today, slightly different behaviours might be necessary to succeed in each of these areas but this is no more than normal rational human behaviour in a free society.

c) Why were Greek practices so different from ours as regards commercial confidentiality and publicity for contracts?

This is the area where Greek practice does differ considerably from that applying now. We have no evidence that the Greeks had a concept of commercial confidentiality. Given the limited evidence that we do have, if the parties themselves had not wished there to be publicised records we would not have had as much evidence as has in fact come down the years to us.

There do not seem to be references, direct or indirect, about confidential contractual deals anywhere in surviving literature. What we do have (but in nearly all cases the evidence is only for what we would now call 'public sector' contracts) are partial records of the terms of contracts on stone (and no doubt at the time many on more perishable materials too), made so that the citizenry could know what contractual deals had been done. The motive may have been initially for accountability, audit and value for money reasons, or it may have been so as to provide an easy

138

to consult working document, but the effect is a public record of contractual deals.

This public record is the opposite of much modern practice, albeit that the EU Public Procurement arrangements, and more recently Freedom of Information legislation, do now demand that a reasonable amount of what thirty years ago was regarded as commercially confidential information should be published. Formal notices of contract intents, and the required debriefing of unsuccessful tenderers under the EU arrangements, do feed back to the marketplace quite a lot of data. However, it is integral to the way our society works that, although on the whole firms welcome the publicity if they have won a contract, they expect confidentiality on what they regard as the 'commercial details', and the whole issue is encompassed by strict legal provisions. One reason for this, of course, is the competitive nature of the technical fixes and techniques modern firms have developed, and which they expect to have protected by Intellectual Property Rights (IPR). There was no concept of IPR as such in the ancient world, although no doubt particular crafts (e.g., carpenters, coopers, masons, metalworkers, pottery makers, sculptors, etc.) all had individually acquired and carefully guarded skill sets, only accessible after selected individuals had served their indentures.

However, I suggest that culturally those who work in business nowadays are expected to have a very different stance to that of the Greeks in respect of their attitude to those not a party to the contract, and it is this, rather than the letter of the law, which is the nub of the matter. I have already mentioned IPR, which can be the most financially important part of a contract, and I suspect the other main factor is the nature of our competitive financial and business driven society. When individuals in business know that to survive (let alone succeed) they have to guard what they know and can do from the next man, they are going to do all they can to control access.

139

In ancient Greece the cultural background was very different. Political and military skills rather than business were the more usual routes to pre-eminence, so 'business', as we tend to know it nowadays, would not necessarily have attracted the most able and ambitious in society. In the political sphere, the (roughly 5th century BCE) societal changes signalled at Athens (at least) by the development of democracy attracted the ambitious, and democracy deliberately increased open systems of government, perhaps in part in reaction to the practices of the pre-democratic ruling systems. Another important factor was that the proportion of panhellenic business and trade that Athens represented was such that its commercial influence was very significant, even among those cities which individually rejected democracy. It follows, therefore, that the Athenian preference for open systems took root in Greek 'public sector' commerce, and perhaps by association rather than by necessity within the wholly 'private sector'.

In present day society, there are always those whose role and way to pre-eminence is to act as Socratic gadflies against the prevailing trend. For example, there are investigative journalists and lawyers, driven either by ambition to right a wrong or to make money from someone else's misfortune (and every position in between these extremes), and those with axes to grind, but for the purposes of the point I am concerned to make, these are the outsiders. The mindset of most people as employees is conditioned by the attitude of their employers, and these are unlikely to see competitive advantage in releasing information unless it is very carefully managed. Furthermore, employees as a whole are driven by the procedures set by their employer, plus the fact that responding to requests for information is yet another imposition on their time. The result is that such information as is issued tends to be as minimal and uninformative as those issuing it think they can get away with. To do otherwise is career limiting.

This is not the place to do more than raise the question whether, if our approach was based on the opposite assumption, namely that everything is made available and transparent, would this of itself beneficially affect the way 'big' business is viewed by the 'ordinary' citizen? I suspect it might, but it is very difficult to see how such a change in emphasis would come about. Already I see armies of lawyers and other professionals, waving cheque books issued by 'big business' and 'vested interests', approaching to stifle such unreliable thoughts. Just because some Greeks, many years ago in entirely different circumstances, did something one way is surely not a realistic way to look at business practice nowadays – or is it? Many of our current difficulties with bankers and politicians (worldwide) relate to the average citizen feeling that others, by virtue of their position in business and society, are doing unfairly well at his expense.

To some extent Greek democracy came about as a response to similar social concerns, and in recent years, whenever failing systems of government have been changed, the banner of democracy and transparency is usually waved by those who think change will improve their lot (for the last 100 or so years often under the guise of communism). Perhaps excessive commercial confidentiality has become, unrecognised probably by many, a WMB – a Weapon of Multinational Business, tending to create or justify potentially divisive social practices. Maybe, in the light of the recent banking crisis (after which the previously accepted norms of late 20th century business life are no longer as apparently acceptable as they once were, and questions have been raised about the social utility of some of the activites of bankers and politicians), an informed debate would now be possible on the real need for some of the commercial confidentiality claims we now almost unthinkingly accept. The alternative, that current trends quietly continue within the relatively closed world of business, risks further alienating public trust in business.

d) Did the Greeks use sub-contractors?

There is plenty of evidence (in the inscriptions and in the orators) of complex webs of obligations, which, even if the term 'sub-contractor' is not used, I suggest are effective proof of broadly analogous practices, and I discussed sub-contracting issues in Chapter 9. Since every man traded as an individual, the sub-contractor concept as we know it is not really relevant, but the evidence is specific – unauthorised sub-letting is explicitly prohibited. When an individual, or numbers of individuals, took responsibility for delivering a major project, we have to assume that ultimately responsibility for delivery remained with the individual, so he would have had to resolve problems if those doing sub-tasks did not deliver.

The structure of projects for temple building, for example, is also evidenced. It seems clear from the epigraphical evidence that at Epidaurus the priests, and later the leading citizens (sometimes the same people), effectively formed a project board and they seem to have placed all the contracts, thus ensuring responsibilities rested directly, as we would say, with the client. But we do not know how the overall plans for the building were drawn up. The situation of e.g., the Acropolis at Athens is perhaps slightly different and probably reflects the inevitable influence of using elite craftsmen/architects. We have the evidence that project boards were set up and reported, but we also know that the master craftsmen/architects Pheidias and Mnesicles took direct responsibility for different works. However, whether they directly took responsibility for all the contracts (we might say as design, manage, build contracting) or whether the Athenian state actually let the contracts (the Epidauran model) we do not know. The evidence of the Arsenal specification – for the whole building – could be taken as meaning one major contract with a single 'architect', i.e. the design, manage, build, model. We have no means of knowing.

e) Were practices such as outsourcing tax collection (tax farming – the 'publicans' of the King James' Bible) the result of a deliberate choice to limit the activities of what we would now call the central bureaucracy, or are there other reasons? Could this be a model for us to follow?

The issue at the heart of this question is the still current debate as to the extent to which governments are able to outsource their critical activities. Currently, in the UK it can be argued that funding public services such as the BBC (through television licences) or roads and bridges by tolls (e.g., the M6 toll road, the Severn Bridge, etc.) are just hypothecated outsourced taxes. VAT itself is an EU-wide way of outsourcing tax collection and one of the reasons for its development was cheapness of collection (by VAT registered businesses trading with each other and across international borders). None of these examples is, however, quite the same as asking a profit-making private sector contractor to collect tax, either for a fee or a commission, from individuals, and there would probably be a political row if a British government were to propose to outsource the collection of, say, income tax, to the private sector by selling off HM Revenue and Customs. The fact that in England too, 300 to 400 years ago, it was the practice for tax revenues to be collected by private individuals, in much the same way as the ancient tax farmers, would not allay the outrage.

Works on Greek public financing have shown that city states were frequently very short of money. In these circumstances those responsible for taxation typically explore all possible ways to raise money and at different times different solutions are found. It may have been that outsourcing tax collection was just seen as the most effective and efficient way of doing this. It is clear that one approach at Athens was for there to be an annual competitive reverse auction: the highest bidder took responsibility for collecting tax from the residents of a particular area. His incentive was the opportunity for large profits from charging the residents exhorbitant sums and having a much smaller sum under contract to pay the state. Despite this drawback, tax farming must have been seen by most citizens as, in principle, an acceptable route for tax collection. We know of nothing to suggest that tax farming of itself was contentious, any more than slavery was, and the two best known references we have to the practice, which are roughly 350-400 years later, and Roman (Cicero's Verrine orations and the biblical references), do not question the principle.

I suggest a possible reason why the ancient practice was different from ours, and why adopting the ancient model as a way of collecting our taxes is probably very difficult to do, is in essence not about principle (though there are some who undoubtedly would consider principles were involved) but simply a matter of self interest arising from an accident of history. In Greece, the social and economic developments of, roughly, the 5th century, meant that a central bureaucracy had to be 'invented' to meet the increasing administrative needs of the state. In Athens, for example, the detailed evidence points to the burgeoning amount of record keeping affecting the role of the Secretary of the Council, so that while the 'political' democratic appointee continued to change, the day-to-day workload was carried out by, in effect, a form of permanent 'civil service'. For the most part, these 'doers' would mainly be slaves, as in societal terms (though not, of course, necessarily in everyday practice) it was the role of the citizen to make the decisions and supervise the process, and for slaves to carry out the work.

In Greece, as citizen numbers changed (mainly tending to reduce unless events persuaded those with this status to widen the franchise) and the numbers of metics and slaves varied according to success or failure in war (a rich source of slaves) or economic prosperity generally, the problem tended to be that over time it became more difficult to find sufficient numbers of people both to manage and carry out the work of tax collection, and indeed other outsourced tasks.

There are many scholarly works which examine the detail of the inscription lists to establish who did what, and others attempt to estimate the populations and resources of the ancient Greeks. My overall impression from these sources is that although, of course, populations rose and declined over time, and there were surpluses and shortages of people in the right places at the right times, overall the Greek city states did not have large surpluses of citizens available to carry out all the tasks needed by the city states. Restrictions on granting the benefits of citizenship (as opposed to lesser status such as a metic or slave) was also a factor.

By contrast, in early 21st century Britain and in general across the EU, there is a long tradition of expecting our taxes to be collected directly by 'the government', and for much of the 20th century until very recently (at least), an expectation that jobs will exist to employ increasing numbers of people, and crucially, large numbers of civil servants, to do long-term public sector roles regardless of economic changes. Outsourcing tax collection, albeit that any contractor would probably merely install new management and take on most of those who actually do the work, would mean major change to parts of the civil services which have existed (in one form or another) for centuries and are perceived by large numbers of employees, and others, as a core function of the state. This would inevitably be seen as a fundamental issue, especially by those accustomed to the state providing services. This does not mean it could not be done.

f) Does the evidence taken as a whole provide information which, if communicated more widely, might have relevance to those dealing with procurement issues now, 2,500 years later?
The very fact that there is evidence that so much of what we now do is so very similar to the way the Greeks did their procurement means that, despite the time and custom distance, they are perhaps

closer to our ways of thinking than we might have expected. It follows that it could be that what they did right, so might we. However, it is very doubtful that the publication of just one more piece of evidence that it should be possible to do procurement better than many now do, will make any difference in itself. But anything which catches the fancy and helps people to think about what they do is useful.

Major project contracting is always extremely difficult. It is undoubtedly easiest to think of parallels in contractual practice in the context of building and civil engineering works. However, this book has also drawn attention to the evidence that we have of very many other types of contractual arrangements, the setting up of which, as even the limited evidence shows, would have required the ancient Greeks to have planned and managed their procurement strategies and addressed problems which, in principle, are similar to those many procurement professionals face today. Maybe what is written here will interest others to explore the evidence in more detail, so different insights may be found.

An area in modern procurement that is still relatively new is the UK's Private Finance Initiative (PFI) and Public Private Partnership (PPP) market, and it may be that a closer study of the ancient evidence will identify helpful pointers as to how the Greeks, who were clearly accustomed to fairly long-term contractual relationships, made them work. For example, there were long-term leases (up to forty years in one case) that the Greeks let for the maintenance of temple sanctuaries. I suspect, however, that even if more detailed study enables a fuller judgment of how it was possible to manage a contract of such a length, the scale and difference of context between a thirty-year build, operate and maintain PPP hospital and what we can find out about maintaining an outsourced Greek temple sanctuary, means that it is difficult to develop the argument beyond two very interesting parallels: (1) that the Greeks developed and used long-term build and maintain contracts; and (2), that the type of structure that appears typically to be managed under this form of contract is often a kind of building associated in the culture of the times with healing. Hospitals (and schools) are often our candidates for PPPs. The arrangements for maintaining religious buildings of architectural and artistic merit vary across the world – many rely ultimately on the state; maybe specifically PPP type contracts would be the answer to their funding problems.

A Concluding Thought

I conclude with the slightly fanciful notion that if modern procurement professionals could travel back 2,500 years in time and were faced with an ancient Greek purchasing project, they might well find Greeks whose approach to the problems would not be entirely different from theirs. It is even possible that our time travellers would come across practices that could foster new insights, or raise questions regarding our current ways of doing business. However, the most fascinating thought is that so little, in total, seems to have changed in terms of procurement technique and practice over the years.

APPENDIX

APPENDIX

AN ANCIENT GREEK CONTRACT

A transliteration of part of a contract (ID502) from the island of Delos, 297BCE, for temple building works. The original broken marble plaque is kept in the Ashmolean Museum, Oxford. It is 0.38 metres high, 0.16 metres long and 0.1m thick and was written on both sides. The style of writing is typical of the time. The transliteration of the surviving writing (see opposite page) was made by the German scholar Ernst Fabricius and was printed with his commentary on the text in the journal *Hermes* (*Hermes* XVII – 1882).

Zu Hermes Bd. XVII S. 1.

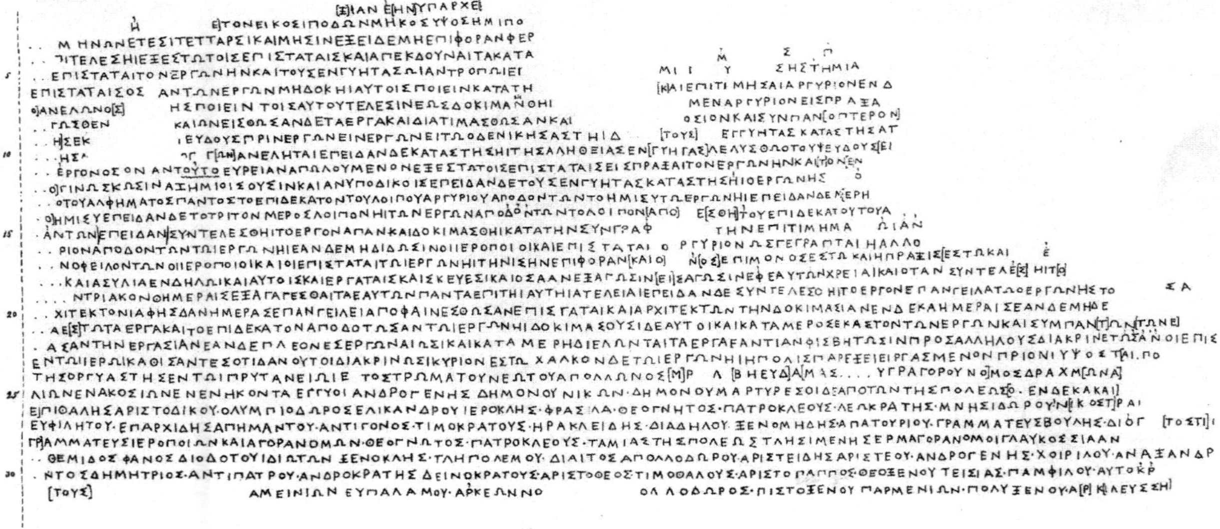

MODERN ENGLISH TRANSLATION OF
THE ANCIENT GREEK CONTRACT

A conjectural free translation, using modern project management terminology whenever it seemed feasible to do so without straining the Greek too far, is set out below. I may have modernised too far for some. For example, the officials known as ἐπιστάται (plural) were overseers of the works, so I have translated as 'Project Committee'. Similarly, the ἱεροποιοι (plural) managed the sacred rites. In this context, I have translated as 'Project Board'. There are also actions placed on the ἀρχιτεκτος (Architect). Another term for him could be 'Project Manager'.

Although quite a lot of this contract document has survived, the top and bottom of the inscription, and the letters at the edges of the inscription are missing, including a substantial portion at the top right. Thus even after scholars have suggested likely words to fill the gaps, there are so many empty spaces that precise word by word translation is impossible. I have mainly left gaps where there is no Greek but have on occasion suggested (in italics) the kind of word we might guess is missing. There are two sections (marked* below) where the sense suddenly appears to change from discussion about a single contract to references to two (or more) contractors. The answer may be that we have specific terms relating to one contract and there was also a section in the inscription which dealt with more general matters, or there was a second contract (the inscription wording also went round the back of the stone but virtually none of the writing there has survived so we do not know what the full text was). None of this detracts from the interest of the material that is clear: information about stage payments, completion and acceptance procedures, guarantors and witnesses to the contract and even embodiment loan, (worked copper was provided).

'.....starts........ 120 feet long, ...half-feet high......................

....

....according to the written contract *for completion within* four years and six months; and if not, *the contractor shall* pay a penalty of ....

.... and if he does not finish the Project Committee has the power both to assign the works that are left and .... Regarding what must be paid the Project Committee .... the contractor and his financial guarantors in whatever manner they can ....

The Project Committee can reject as much of the works as seems to them not to be in accordance with the written contract and they must provide their assessment of value within ten days. But the contractor is required to complete the works if this is the best solution.

The Project Committee .... the money to be paid ....

....

...... and they shall accept the works and make an assessment of value of .... the temple and state property and everything ....

*{*The next section is very difficult. It looks as if it is about the importance of contractors obtaining the work properly and using appropriately established and genuine guarantors. If this provision is not kept the client has the right to repudiate the contract and seek other contractors.*
Perhaps it was something like:

Let each man compete for the work in a just way before the contract starts and not give false promises. The winner in the competition must appoint guarantors of his good faith against the risk of falsehoods .... before there is expenditure under the contract. When guarantors of good faith are established, anyone who has obtained work under false promises shall be released from the contract .... and a search to find another contractor shall be made.}

The Project Committee must insist that the contractor and his guarantors enter into .... if they have advance knowledge, being without penalties and without further liabilities.

After the contractor has appointed the guarantors .... the Project Board and Project Committee can call down a 10% deposit from the full contract sum and assign half of the remaining money for the contractor; and when two sections remain of the works they may assign 50% of it and when the remaining third only is left they may assign the rest. ....the 10% deposit having been subtracted from the contract sum.

When the whole works shall come to an end a final assessment valuation shall be made in accordance with this written contract, and after a value has been placed on any work rejected the remaining money shall be paid to the contractor. If the Project Board and Committee do not make the payment as the written contract says, or they do not stand by their full responsibilities, the members of the Project Board and Committee themselves will owe the due amount to the contractor, and though there will be a delay of the payment the transaction will stand. The contractor and his team and workforce and equipment will be granted freedom from taxes and liabilities in Delos in respect of import and export rights for their own use. When all the work is completed, they will be given 30 days to export all their equipment and personal effects without being subject to taxation.

When all the work is completed, the contractor shall notify the Project Committee and Architect that he has completed and from that point the Project Committee and Architect shall make it known that the final assessment valuation will take place within 10 days. If they do not carry out the final asessment valuation within 10 days the works shall be deemed assessed and the 10% deposit paid to the contractor. And they personally shall carry out the final assessment valuation both separately on each part of the works and as a whole on everything that has been done as part of the contract.

*And if a number of contractors press and insist the works be assessed section by section or if they dispute with each other, the Project Committee shall settle the matter formally in the temple and their judgement shall be final.

The city will provide copper for the Contractor which has been worked with a one and a half foot long saw, as measured by the official measuring rod in the Town Hall.

.... This contract was made on the pavement of the temple of Apollo between the City and Damasias, son of Kupragoros of Paros, for the sum of 970,000 silver drachmas. Andromenes, son of Demonos and Nikos, son of Demonos were financial guarantors. The witnesses were: For the City, the Eleven and the Secretary Epithales son of Aristodikos, Olympiodoros son of Hellikandros, Leoncrates son of Mnesidoros, etc., etc., etc.....
[The list of named officials is extensive, as is customary.]

SELECT BIBLIOGRAPHY

Books and articles

Archibald, Z H, Davies, J K, and Gabrielsen, V, *Making, Moving and Managing the New World of Ancient Economies 323-31BC* (Oxbow, 2005).

Behrend, D, *Attische Pachturkunden* (Munchen, 1971).

Bresson, A, *La Cité Marchande* (Ausonius, 2000).

Bresson, A, *L'economie de la Grece des Cités* (1): *Les structures et la production* (Armand Colin 2008).

Broome, J, *Procurement Routes to Partnering – A Practical Guide* (Thomas Telford, 2002).

Burford, A, *The Greek Temple Builders at Epidaurus* (Liverpool, 1969).

Cartledge, P, Cohen, E, and Foxhall, L, *Money, Labour and Land* (Routledge, 2002).

Contract Management Guide – CIPS (Published on www.cips.org.uk, 2007).

Feyel, C, *Les artisans dans les sanctuaires grecs aux époques classique et hellénistique á travers la documentation financière en Grec* (De Boccard, 2006).

Gauthier, P, *Symbola* (Nancy, 1972).

Guest (ed.) in *Anson's Law of Contract*, 21st Edition (Oxford, 1959).

Harris, W V, *The Monetary Systems of the Greeks and Romans* (OUP, 2008).

Harris, E M, *When is a sale not a sale?* (CQ 38, 1988, pp. 351-381); *Liability of Athenian business partners in Athenian Law* (CQ 39, 1989, pp. 339-393); *Athenian Terminology for Real Security* (CQ 43, 1993 pp. 73ff).

Jones, J Walter, *Law and Legal theory of the Greeks* (Oxford, 1956).

Lysons, K, and Farrington, B, *Purchasing and Supply Management*, 7th edition (Pearson Education, 2006).

Meijer and Van Nijf, *Trading, Transport and Society in the Ancient World – A sourcebook* (Routledge, 1992).

Migeotte, L, *L'emprunt public dans les cités greques* (Paris, 1984).

Millett, P, in *Trade in the Ancient Economy*, Ed. P Garnsey et al ii 1-15 (Berkeley, 1983).

Observer Newspaper 25th January 2009 – Views of Head of British Library about information published only on websites.

Osborne, R, *Social and Economic Implications of the Leasing of Land and Property in Classical and Hellenistic Greece* (Chiron 18, 1988, pp. 278-323).

Pringsheim, F, *Greek Law of Sale* (Weimar, 1950).

Reed, C M, *Maritime traders in the Ancient Greek World* (CUP, 2003).

Reger, G, *Regionalism and Change in the Economy of Independent Delos* (1985).

Report by the Comptroller and Auditor General, Central Government's Management of Service Contract (December 2008).

Sanchez, P, *L'Amphictionie des Pyles et de Delphes* (Stuttgart, 2001).

Seaford, R, *Money and the Early Greek Mind* (Cambridge, 2004).

Shipton, K, *Leasing and Lending in Fourth Century BC Athens* (ICT London, 2000).

Sickinger, J P, *Public records and archives in Classical Athens* (University of N. Carolina, 1999).

Somolinos, H R, *The Commercial Transaction of the Pech Maho Lead: A New Interpretation* Zeitschrift fur Papyrologie und Epigraphik 111 (1996) pp. 48-74, Bonn.

Thompson, W E, *The Athenian Entrepreneur* (Antique Classique 51, pp. 53-85).

SELECT BIBLIOGRAPHY

Alphabetical list of ancient authors referred to (Loeb or Penguin edition translations, when available, generally used for short quotations)

Andocides
Aristotle
Aristophanes
Demosthenes
Herodotos
Hyperides
Isocrates
Isaeus
Lycurgus
Lysias
Plato
Plutarch
Stobaeus Anthology (for Theophrastos)
Thucydides
 Xenophon
Virgil
Vitruvius

The online Greek inscriptions recorded in the Princeton Epigraphical Project proved to be a very convenient means of accessing epigraphical material which was usually first identified from other reading, such as the *Inscriptiones Graecae* series, *Syllogium Epigraphicae Graecae* series, etc., and collections such as Pieket, Rhodes and Osborne, Thir und Tauber, etc.